SCANDINAVIAN
PAINTED DECOR

SCANDINAVIAN PAINTED DECOR

JOCASTA INNES

PHOTOGRAPHY BY
DAVID GEORGE

RIZZOLI
NEW YORK

First published in the United States of America in 1990 by
Rizzoli International Publications, Inc.
300 Park Avenue South, New York, NY 10010

Library of Congress Cataloging-in-Publication Data

Innes, Jocasta.
    Scandinavian painted decor/Jocasta Innes
photography by David George
    p.   cm.
    ISBN 0-8478-1235-9
    1. Mural painting and decoration–Scandinavia.   2. Painted
woodwork–Scandinavia.   3. Decoration and ornament–
Scandinavia–Themes, motives.   4. Mural painting and decoration–
Baltic States.   5. Painted woodwork–Baltic States.   6. Decoration
and ornament–Baltic States–Themes, motives.   I. Seamark,
Roger.   II. Title.
ND2770.155   1990
729'.4'0948–dc20   90-31550
                                                                          CIP

Printed and bound in Italy

FRONTISPIECE PICTURE *The beautiful lilacs, greens and
blues of this interior from Skogaholm Manor at Skansen
in Stockholm, faded over the years, pick up the natural
tones of the wood but belie their own original bright
beginnings.*

CONTENTS

INTRODUCTION

Stretching like a roomy mysterious attic under the eaves of the world, Scandinavia has been taking travellers by surprise since Pliny, the Roman historian, recorded – with a tremor of wonderment breaking through his matter-of-fact style – that 'immense islands had of late been discovered, beyond Germany, and of these the noblest was Scandinavia, of yet unknown magnitude: the inhabitants styled it another world.' The inhabitants, mark. If Scandinavia has appeared peripheral, historically, to classical culture centred on the Mediterranean, the Scandinavian races, too, have been deeply conscious of their isolation. Geographically, Scandinavia is a cul-de-sac, on the road to nowhere but the old enemy, Russia, across the Baltic Sea.

Today, despite the abundant evidence that the four countries designated Scandinavian (Denmark, Sweden, Norway, Finland) are among the most prosperous and progressive in the modern world, despite Scandinavian influences in the language and history of English-speakers, despite the Scandinavian exports woven into our daily existence, Scandinavia still deals out surprises to a first-time visitor. The culture shock is subtle, persistent and unexpected.

The 'magnitude' of these countries is the first surprise to the newcomer. Sweden is the size of California, its slender length (it is not unlike the fatter half of a split herring in shape, separated by a mountainous spine from Norway) punctured by 96,000 lakes, bristling with 50 million, or is it a billion, trees. Finland, extending like a lintel resting on Sweden and Russia, has an even greater proportion of its surface covered by trees and water (its lakes are picturesquely referred to as 'the blue eyes of Finland') – so much so that it is a puzzle to see where the population found a toehold. Denmark, a cluster of islands at the

Completed in 1780, the Amalienborg, in Copenhagen, is one of Scandinavia's most remarkable architectural set pieces. Denmark's Royal family today lives in one or other of the four identical stone mansions which stand facing each other, linked by colonnades, across as a mighty sweep of cobbles on an axis between the domed bulk of the 'Marmorkirke' or 'marble church' on the one hand, and the tranquil quays of Amaliehaven on the other.

7

ABOVE *A Nordic dandy in bronze, the swashbuckling figure of Danish nineteenth-century poet, Adam Oelenschlager, stands before a pleached lime allee in Copenhagen's Sondermarken park, looking out towards Frederiksberg Slott, the former Royal Palace, where he was a frequent visitor. The vivid blue-green patination which salt air and a Scandinavian climate lends to public statuary and metalwork is one of the incidental beauties of northern cities, in colourful contrast to russet and ochre limewash, dark brickwork, mellow stone, or, as here, the breathcatching colours of autumn.*

OPPOSITE *Demure as a doll's house beyond clipped box parterres and gravelled walks, the elegant little manor house of Beatelund, on the Stockholm archipelago, exhibits such typically Scandinavian features as a* sateri *(stepped roof), pale limewashed walls, and an overall air of ordered symmetry. The present building dates from 1719, and contains fine painted hangings and grisaille ceilings of the period.*

toe of Sweden augmented by the long sandy tongue of Continental Europe called Jutland, is flat, fertile land, remarkably like the east coast of Britain where the Danish raiders in their longships made landfall a thousand years or so ago. But it is only when travelling across the Scandinavian landscape that its real scale becomes apparent. Fast trains, excellent roads, shuttle air services, regular ferry boats enable the traveller to move rapidly over long distances, yet a visitor is constantly aware of the apparently unpopulated terrains lying outside the busy communication network. Forest, water and thin soil cover a granite skeleton, which erupts here and there in outcrops of boulders, pinkish and speckled, extending northwards to the snowline where the Lapps live.

The character of the landscape and, above all, the vivid, unexpected colourfulness of its towns and villages, are perhaps the greatest surprise Scandinavia keeps, as it were, up her capacious sleeves. The chief Scandinavian cities, Stockholm, Gothenburg, Oslo, Copenhagen, Helsinki, smoulder beside their watery setting with a Venetian warmth and richness of tone, modulating from cool cream, through a crescendo of ochre, apricot, amber and salmon pink, to a sumptuous coda of russet and the deeper red known as *sang de boeuf*, or less poetically, as maroon. Jumbled together in a stretch of old house fronts, these limewash colours sing out, mingling as harmoniously as a bunch of wallflowers.

In the northern latitudes, the long winter of sub-zero temperatures and niggardly northern light, dwindling to a few pallid hours between long stretches of darkness, weighs oppressively upon the Scandinavian consciousness. Today there are special psychotherapy units where sufferers from depression induced by light deprivation are treated; the cause is diagnosed as deficiency of sunshine vitamins, and the treatment consists of exposure to ultra-violet light in measured doses. But what is less obvious, and can only perhaps be sensed on the spot, is the range and variety of the *psychological* defences that the inhabitants of the Nordic countries have created and used to fortify themselves against the bleak winter darkness. Colour and light, historically, seem to have been spiritual fuel to a degree which no-one today, living in a world surfeited with visual images and homes cocooned and buffered against cold and darkness, can easily imagine. Light, from whatever source, was not something to be taken for granted, but husbanded and magnified. Just as the first sunshine fills Scandinavian parks with goosepimpled sunbathers, the first hint of approaching winter – even today – is warded off by a blaze of candles. Santa Lucia, the ceremony where young girls parade wearing crowns of evergreen spiked with candles, is surely a pagan ceremony in Christian dress. Anyone who has visited many old buildings in Scandinavia cannot fail to notice the diversity and elegance of their light enhancers, from the simple lanterns hanging from castle walls, to the glittering fountains of crystal drops which hang from privileged ceilings and sprout like tiny frosted trees in the form of girandoles and lustres. Peasants relied chiefly on firelight, although they made their own tapers and rushlights, as elsewhere, from rushes dipped in tallow and string suspended in beeswax. The scarcity and luxury of such forms of lighting can be gauged

Dapper as sharp new pencils, these little sentry boxes provide shelter for Royal Lifeguards on guard duty in Amalienborg, the great cobbled piazza where Queen Margrethe, the Queen Mother and Crown Prince live in one or other of the four fine stone mansions cutting across the corners of a square site to form an octagon centred upon a spirited equestrian statue of Frederik V.

from old records of victuals and other benefits allowed to the 'statt drangarne' or victualled servants of noble households in Sweden. Whereas the annual provision of food might include sixty pounds of dried beef, a bushel of hops, nine gallons of salt (for salting down and preserving meat and fish), plus a daily allowance of quarts of new and soured milk, their Christmas bonus stretched, amid pecks of rye and pints of brandy, to just one medium-sized candle.

If light, being precious, was hoarded, colour, being cheaper and more permanent, was splashed about with an intensity and fervour that make a visitor's eyes pop in startled amazement. The exultant polychrome decoration of medieval churches outstrips the tamer imaginings of people to whom colour historically was a pleasure rather than a craving. Even when the colours have been faded by centuries of exposure, the adjective that immediately comes to mind is psychedelic. This is colour used as an intoxicant, deliriously invading every last surface in a blaze of defiance.

With prosperity and progress this ancient greed for colour seems to have been driven underground. There is a tameness, a kind of pastel-shaded timidity, about most contemporary Scandinavian interior decoration that seems surprising given the abundance of surviving traditional painted decoration. However, there are reasons why modern Scandinavians might fight shy of the adventurous colour feasts of their ancestors. The peasant past may still be too recent, in some respects, to be ransacked for inspiration as blithely as current designers in Europe and the United States raid old textile patterns in museum archives. Then there was the Modern Movement, which launched Scandinavian architects of world renown, such as Asplund, Alvar Aalto, and Utzon, who designed the Sydney Opera House. World stature is something that counts for much in countries where the Great Power period of Swedish history is still wryly referred to, two centuries later, as their one moment of glory on the world stage, when they were taken seriously into the reckonings of scheming statesmen and monarchs elsewhere in Europe. For centuries, travellers' tales from Scandinavia put about the most patronizing accounts of life in Pliny's 'immense islands', either dwelling upon their barbarism, or exclaiming in astonishment over their comparative civilization. One captures the tone immediately from the travelogue by Sir John Carr published in 1805, who gleefully recounts of the late King Charles XII of Sweden that 'the king never used a comb but his fingers, and used to butter his bread with his thumb'. Moreover, that the breeches worn by Charles when he was killed in battle in 1718 'were so greasy they may be fried'. More than two centuries earlier, it is recounted by contemporary writers that Queen Elizabeth I, on being petitioned for her hand in marriage on behalf of Erik, unstable heir to the great Gustavus I Vasa of Sweden, suddenly flew into a towering rage and forbade any further mention of this upstart suitor.

It would hardly be surprising if, after centuries of being treated as uncouth barbarians with revolting table manners, the proud inhabi-

Turf roofs are a common sight in Scandinavia, especially in northern Sweden, but the emerald-green growth seen here is a thick carpet of moss overlaying an old thatched roof in a hamlet on the Danish island of Fyn. Note the hemispherical dormer window neatly scooped out of the thatch. Thatched roofs and half timbering are two characteristics shared by many cottages in this flat and fertile countryside with counterparts in East Anglia where so many Danish settlements grew up during the early medieval period.

tants of the Scandinavian countries became eager to appear more modern and progressive than their neighbours. Modern Scandinavians give the impression of being so intent on keeping ahead, or at least abreast, of the rest of the world, that they appear to have lost contact with their past. And yet to the visitor this past seems very close, persisting just beneath the skin of shiny modern life and liable to manifest itself suddenly in the form of, for instance, a wooden cottage at the foot of a glass and steel office block. Within the wooden cottage is a time capsule where everything looks much as it would have done one, two, even three hundred years ago.

This is true of Scandinavian buildings at every level of splendour. Part of the excitement of discovering these seemingly untouched interiors (and the interiors are somehow more evocative than the exteriors) is that they often fill gaps in our knowledge of our own architectural and social history. Terse contemporary accounts of medieval decorated interiors, rubble walls and mullioned windows painted white and lined in red, to imitate dressed stone blocks, fail to excite the imagination; but inside a Swedish castle, with whitewashed masonry, and red ornament doodled round windows and doorways, or in a Danish castle, where elaborately chequered walls meet massive roof beams painted red, the medieval world comes closer. Visual surprises march with every architectural period: complete window treatments – drapes, bobble fringes and gilt crescents – from the early nineteenth century, while from the seventeenth and eighteenth centuries come alcove beds of amazingly cramped dimensions hung with their original sprigged print curtains; baroque marbling of hectic colouring, resembling jellied brawn; the daintiest filigree cut-out paper pictures; the whitewashed beams of Skokloster castle outlined in watery sugared almond colours; carved and studded wooden front doors picked out in red and blue and white, and window blinds painted with pots of flowers on the street side, so that, when pulled down, the housefront presents a cheerful, symmetrical face to the passers by.

Yet there is more to this visual feast than mere charm or cheerfulness. There are powerful forces at work in the fierce energy of early Norwegian church painting, with its overtones of Viking paganism – the same forces which have sent armies on the march in a long and complex history of conflict, conquest and reconquest among the Scandinavian countries themselves. With its many dialects of the three main languages, its far-flung communities and formidable barriers of mountain, water and forest, Scandinavia has often been fragmented – but in ways which have tended to reinforce a stubborn independence at every level from the rural peasantry to city burgesses, from country gentry to the turbulent aristocracy. Distinctive local traditions, tenaciously held and slow to change, provide the richness of the Scandinavian heritage of traditional painted decoration – but the bright colours could perhaps be seen as war-flags too. And that may be another reason why the neutral Scandinavia of the twentieth century has embraced the cooler Modernist shades of blue, grey and blond.

THE TREE OF LIFE:
WOOD CULTURE IN SCANDINAVIA

Yggdrasil, the cosmic tree of Norse mythology, whose roots descend to the underworld and whose topmost branches scrape the stars, is as vivid a representation as one could hope to find of the crucial importance of trees and their products to Scandinavian life. In earlier times forest trees really were, as the old Swedish proverb has it, 'the poor man's winter shirt'. Even more than shelter and warmth, trees supplied most of the needs of daily life from cradle to coffin. The majority of the population lived in wooden or timber-framed houses, with wooden furniture and wooden utensils – from the trough where bread dough was kneaded, to the bowls, plates and spoons for everyday use. People wore clogs made of alder wood, and worked with wooden tools – ploughs, harrows, spinning wheels, looms. Wood supplied them with sleds and boats for travel and transport. In times of famine trees even provided starving peasants with food. Bark bread, made by peeling, drying and pulverizing the membrane just beneath the bark to make a floury substance, did more than fill hungry stomachs; according to the twentieth-century writer Vilhelm Moberg, it contained some protein and was rich in minerals. Its flavour, he reports, is insipid, a little sour.

Finland, northern Sweden and parts of Norway comprise the most densely forested areas of Scandinavia. In Finland what is not lake – and there are 60,000 of these – is forest. Southern Sweden and Denmark used to be rich in oaks and beeches, slow-growing deciduous trees that need more fertile soil and a milder climate but, as in England and elsewhere, these ancient forests dwindled rapidly after the Middle Ages. For several centuries now most timber for building, paper making, and so on, has come from the north; it used to be floated down-river by melting snow water in spring. Most Scandinavian forest is naturally mixed, with conifers gradually ousting deciduous trees,

Traditional wooden utensils, like this staved lidded beerstoup bound with strips of willow, are splendid, gutsy objects, eloquent of the rural culture which crafted and used them habitually. They may look primitive but when well made they were strong and serviceable, outlasting ceramics, mellowing with use. A lidded tankard like this was used to bring ale from the cellar. This was decanted into smaller tankards with spouts, the drinkers drinking from the spouts rather than the rim. Wooden utensils for special occasions – drinking bowls, porringers, cheese and butter moulds – were usually decorated with carved, painted or burnt-in patterns.

Aside from the textiles and brass oil lamp, everything in this peasant interior is wooden, the building itself, the furniture, built-in or free-standing. A cupboard has been attached to the end partition of the built-in bed, and a long bench runs along the window wall behind the standard long wooden table where families would work – eking out natural daylight from the windows – as well as eat. Families higher up the social scale had separate bedrooms; peasants continued to live, eat, sleep and work in one large room. But as the wall and ceiling decorations show, this small farm was prosperous enough to aspire to afford more than the bare rudiments.

OPPOSITE *Falun red for the walls of a stuga which protects itself against foul weather with massive shutters stained with creosote. Nowadays all stuga windows, however small or shuttered, would also have double, even triple, glazing.*

14

mostly birch, maple and aspen, as one travels northwards. In autumn, when the deciduous leaves turn a clear, translucent yellow and red more brilliant than Viking gold or copper, the great undulating stretches of forest on all sides go piebald, the sombre green of conifers patched and blotched with flaring colour. 'I have become solitary,' says the bereaved Gudrun of the saga, 'like an aspen among the evergreens.'

Softwoods – all from conifers – are paradoxically more difficult to work than hardwoods, although results come more quickly when the appropriate techniques are used. In fact, wood-working skills were always advanced in the Nordic countries, and the sophistication of Viking carpentry can be seen from the variety of techniques for slotting timber boards together in use by the eleventh century. Modern tongue-and-groove construction looks rudimentary compared with some of these interlocking devices. Presumably the chief purpose behind them was to make walls which were weatherproof and sturdy, but they must also have produced handsome surfaces, rugged or smooth as the situation demanded.

A once-painted barn door latched to a plank wall treated with Falun red provides an extraordinary study in rugged, weathered wood texture.

Rooms like these were built and decorated by the more prosperous peasantry expressly for festive and ceremonious family occasions: weddings, name days, christenings, but also funerals and the laying-out of the dead for family and neighbours to pay their respects. Though the furnishing is basic, it is all of a certain elegance, painted white like the boarded ceiling to maximize light – provided at night by candles in wall corners and by the alarmingly low-slung chandelier. But of course it is the sprightly and colourful wall paintings, in the kurbits style, which dress up the room and transform it into party mood. These particular hangings are of exceptional quality, among the more finely painted and best preserved in Sweden.

One consequence of the care and skill which went into making buildings solid and watertight is that even the smallest wooden cottage has a well-made look. Doors, steps, porches are solidly made, and decently finished. Internal joinery shares these qualities; everything from the tightly laid floorboards to the built-in furnishings has a generous air about it. Sometimes the design is awkward, or crude, but nothing wooden appears skimped or flimsy. Wood is an extraordinarily sympathetic material; used throughout an interior it gives warmth and dignity to the poorest room. But the use of wood as a basic building material has given all types of traditional Scandinavian architecture a special character. A wooden house, however large and imposing, always retains a degree of rusticity, a friendliness inherent in the material. Some of the most attractive buildings in Scandinavia, to a modern eye, are the eighteenth- and early nineteenth-century country mansions and manor houses, which attempt the style of a Palladian or neo-classical stone or brick villa in wood. From a distance the illusion holds; the *slott* or *herrgård* standing out in all its yellow and white paint as conspicuous and confident as the great pillared and porticoed English Palladian mansions of the same period. But there is a subtle difference, an absence of monumentality, which grows more pronounced as one approaches. As soon as it becomes apparent that these houses, elegant and decorous though they may be, are faced with timber cladding, their impressiveness disappears; instead of intimidating they somehow cannot help looking friendly and approachable. The special charm which attends provincial attempts at the grand style is nowhere more beguiling than in these wooden mansions trying to pass for stone and stucco.

ABOVE *Wood carving has been one expression of Scandinavian woodcraft since Viking times, only a little hampered by the comparative difficulty of carving into soft and brittle conifer rather than hard-grained woods like oak. The carved chair shown here is made, unusually, from oak, and this is reflected in the greater complexity of the decoration. The woeful faces carved on the arms could have been lifted from medieval choir stalls.*

RIGHT *Renaissance pieces like this carved oak cupboard from Nyborg Slott, in Denmark, were often decorated with carved patterns in low relief which were then picked out in vivid colours. Traces of red and green can be seen on this piece.*

More town house than country manor, this trim neo-classical wooden building from the north-eastern Swedish town of Gävle nevertheless shares many of the features which make late eighteenth-century wooden manors and stately homes so appealing compared with their grander relations in stone, brick or stucco. Pale yellow and white paintwork is the Gustavian formula intended to suggest stone and stucco. The neat pediment pierced with a round window, like the applied pilasters (which are merely more boards, three at a time), have obvious neo-classical aspirations, while the iron balcony doubles as a porch for the front door below. The charm and essential modesty of timber cladding survive even where the house in question is a greatly magnified version of this small town house. American readers will recognize a prototype of one of their own most attractive housing types, the neat and dignified, but also homely and approachable, houses which line the streets of so many east-coast towns in the United States.

PAINTS AND PIGMENTS

More than most people outside conservationist circles realize, the strikingly atmospheric quality of Scandinavian painted decoration is due to the use of traditional paints, technologically primitive but pure, as well as to what seems an innate skill in making up distinctive colours and combining them effectively. Until the advent of vinyl-based (latex) paint in the 1950s brought home decorating within the scope of anyone who could wield a brush and open a can of paint, all Scandinavian interior and exterior paints were made up on the spot using traditional recipes and ingredients, which in many cases had scarcely altered for hundreds of years.

What this conservatism with paint contributed to the characteristic look of towns and cities can be gauged by comparing old buildings, still finished in traditional paint and colours, with more recent structures, which are usually coated with modern commercial paints. Aside from the ubiquitous Falun red, which is discussed elsewhere, the prevalent external finish on these old buildings is limewash or *kalkmålning* (literally – chalk painting) in a subtle range of colours from creamy ochre, through tawny orange with a greenish astringency, to potent salmon pinks, russets and a velvety maroon. All these colours are obtained by mixing the restricted range of pigments, mostly earth colours, which are viable in limewash. The limewash base makes an additional contribution to the colour by giving a transparency, liveliness and an inner glow to the pigment mixed with it. The result is a clear and pure colour that is quite different from the inert opacity of modern vinyl paints. Limewash colours have a vitality that lights up a street or square: they are also organic paints that allow the surfaces to 'breathe', a practical reason for their continued use on officially protected, or

Frugal as it is, this room in an old rope-maker's cottage in a Stockholm back street is rich in atmosphere, an elusive quality but one into which the mystery of colour, reticent here but haunting, undoubtedly enters. The puttyish colour of woodwork and chairs sets up a pleasing relationship with the serene pallor of scrubbed boards, but what makes this little vignette of Scandinavian domesticity so distinctively of its own place and time is the spread of subtle blue paint across the hallway beyond, a blue characteristic of Scandinavian interiors at all social levels, and intimately bound up with the all-pervasive blues of sea, lakes, and sky.

ABOVE *A special delight of Scandinavian cities, Copenhagen especially, is the pungency of exterior limewash colours like the traditional shade, tawny-orange but with the softness of mangoes rather than the hardness of oranges, which is shown here dappling the walls of stables and other outbuildings to Denmark's celebrated Helsingör Castle, where Shakespeare set the action of Hamlet. Many old buildings in Copenhagen are painted with this peculiarly fine-tuned limewash colour which manages to be vibrant and exhilarating, without harshness. The Scandinavians tend to mix the shade today, using the recipe given in this chapter, but older formulations available in Britain from conservationist-minded companies make use of tinting compounds based on by-products of copper manufacturing, often called Copperas.*

merely old, Scandinavian buildings. Commercial paint firms have come up with colours that approximate to the limewash colours – creams, yellows, pinks and so forth – but the chemical constituents that allow easy application and a uniform colour have a deadening effect on reflectivity. Limewash colours seem to change constantly according to the light: they fade in bright sunlight, darken in rain and gently weather over the years.

Traditional limewash colours used in Scandinavia are all beautiful, but perhaps the most unusual and memorable to a visitor is the glowing, but never garish, tawny orange that is used all over Scandinavia, but nowhere, for some reason, quite so vividly as in Denmark, where it gives such a distinctive coppery radiance to the Royal stables, and the old buildings surrounding Kronborg Castle (Shakespeare's Elsinore), among others. The shade is composed of a mixture of yellow ochre and a little Venetian red and white. The more layers of coloured limewash that are applied, the more intense the basic hue becomes, and this may explain why the Danish version is so vivid, as the Danes repaint their buildings more often. Limewash can be painted straight on to wood and in the past was often used over half-timbered buildings, both inside and out, as a combined paint and preservative, the mildly caustic properties of slaked lime acting as a deterrent to woodworm and deathwatch beetle. It is also possible to apply limewash over modern emulsion paints provided they are first sealed with size.

The traditional limewash technique in Scandinavia is what is known elsewhere as *fresco secco* – that is, painting on to a dry plastered wall. True fresco, in which the pigments are ground into wet plaster, which is then rendered onto moist plaster, is not found. For *fresco secco*, lime, the basic constituent, was extracted by burning limestone to yield a white powder, which was then slaked in water, and usually purveyed commercially in the form of lime paste or putty. Limewater was made by soaking lime putty in water, in varying proportions. A surface was prepared for *al secco* painting by washing over a lime-rendered surface, with successively stronger concentrations of lime water, which is liquid that forms on top of the soaked lime. Uncoloured, this surface dries to a dazzling white, the finish seen on vernacular buildings all over the Mediterranean. For coloured limewash, lime-proof pigments are added to the liquid (these include all the earth colours, also iron-oxide colours, ultramarine, lamp black, crome-oxide green, and cobalt, and to a lesser degree, cobalt green, blue copper carbonates, and cadmium colours) and test samples are left to dry over several days for the final colours to develop. The painted surfaces needed to be protected against drying either too fast or too slowly, which meant screening off direct sunlight, and protecting them from frost in the first few weeks after they had been completed. In a Scandinavian climate this restriction would have limited the fresco painting season to about six months of the year.

OPPOSITE *More of the same tawny orange limewash, counterpointed by a mysterious blackish-green prevalent throughout Northern Europe, gives alluring warmth to this side street in old Stockholm, the Gamla Stan or Old Town, where seventeenth- and eighteenth-century survivals include wooden shutters and tautly elegant ironwork.*

This detail of one of Stockholm's older quarters gives some idea of the almost Venetian warmth of colouring of so many Scandinavian towns and cities.

OPPOSITE *Exterior colours in Scandinavia have to hold their own in a climate which see-saws between extremes, the freshest of spring leafiness, the starkness of winter snow. These plain but pleasing old timber-clad houses, fronting a street in the northerly Swedish town of Gävle, are painted in typical colours – the dull pinks and genial ochres which contrast well with a snowy foreground.*

Despite the undeniable beauty of the *fresco secco* techniques, decorative painters were naturally interested in other techniques that could give a similar effect for less trouble. *Limfarg*, or distemper, was made from cheap, readily available ingredients and gave strong, clear, matt colours. It was the most widely used paint for domestic purposes throughout Scandinavia for almost a thousand years, and was still being used on hand-printed wallpapers as late as 1960. Scandinavian painters not only went on using this primitive but visually pleasing paint for longer than most Europeans, but they seem to have amassed a great deal of precise information on such subtleties as which glue binder gave best results under different circumstances. Nordic painters were travelling journeymen seeking work where they could find it, making use of locally available materials. This might mean using rye flour with casein (usually in the form of buttermilk) to make an extremely tough exterior and interior paint; beer and vinegar as glazes for graining and marbling, and animal blood and the juice of loganberries and blueberries as tinting agents.

Basic distemper was made from powdered chalk or whiting, water, size (thinned animal glue) and dry colour in the form of powdered pigment. Chalk was poured into a bucket of water till a cone of powder showed above the water level. This was left to soak overnight, without stirring. The size, usually bone or rabbit-skin glue in crystal form, was also left to soak overnight in a separate container of water. The next day the size and water mixture was heated until the crystals were completely dissolved; it was then added to the chalk and water and thoroughly mixed. Today, conservationists find that an electric drill with a propeller attachment is ideal for blending these heavy ingredients together, but in the old days this was a task needing a good deal of elbow grease. Straight from the bucket, distemper is a warm white. Any pigments to be added need to be dissolved first in warm water. Some 'fatty' pigments dissolve more easily if a teaspoon of methylated spirits is added. Distemper colours dry paler than when wet. Because of its chalk content it is easy to mix pastel shades of distemper, which have a soft but intense tone. For strong or dark colours, a great deal of dry colour has to be substituted for the chalk; in former times these would have been relatively expensive decorating colours.

Various different glues were used to make distemper: they were all organic, and mostly derived from animals although carageen and rye or potato starch were sometimes used as well. Parchment size, made from animal skins, usually rabbit skin, was the most expensive and the most efficient binder, holding the chalk so that it did not rub off easily, the common problem with distemper. It also gave the dry paint a soft shimmer. Bone glue was a less powerful binder, but it, too, gave a shimmer to the paint. Carageen, a form of red seaweed, produces a flaky distemper that was only used for ceilings. Distemper was usually brushed on quite thickly with a wide brush used in one direction only, but it could also be stippled, sponged or spattered on to give different textures. Despite its tendency to flake and rub it was frequently used for murals, and for marbling in modest homes, on wood and log walls as well as plastered ones. Some of the Norwegian stave churches were decorated in distemper, coloured red, yellow or black, like the Viking

ABOVE *Traditional paints age differently from modern equivalents, eroding or frittering away with dignity. The texture of these old, worn surfaces is often beautiful, eloquent of use and gentle disrepair.*

rune stones, and it was also used for the most primitive form of decoration in peasant homes in Norway, the *kroting* borders of geometric patterns which the women of the family used to paint along the topmost log of their log walls like a strip of embroidery. Almost all the vernacular decorated effects shown in this book are painted in distemper.

Considering the medium's relative fragility, a quite remarkable number of early Scandinavian distempered interiors have survived and distemper, along with many other traditional 'organic' finishes, is steadily becoming more popular in Scandinavia, helped by the influence of the green movement. Distemper paints are being adopted by people who value its ecological soundness as well as its soft powdery bloom and intense colours.

Another traditional, but much more expensive, finish was egg tempera, an emulsion made by combining egg yolk, linseed oil and water with dry pigment. This ancient form of paint has a delicate translucent quality and, although it takes a long time to dry hard, is exceptionally durable. Its chief use seems to have been in furniture painting and decoration and, latterly, in the delicate rendering of ornament on the painted canvas wall-hangings called *tapeter*, especially the garlanded fillets so popular in the rococo period and later. The status of egg

RIGHT *A wider view of the same* stuga *doorway in the north-western Swedish province of Värmland shows just how ineffable the colouring of old, weathered home-made paints becomes as they age, peeling off here and there but retaining a subtle bloom of colour – here, the red-brown seen everywhere in rural Sweden, balanced against a subtle but faded sap green and the chalky white of wooden posts and railings.*

tempera – as neat, natural and durable – remains high in Scandinavia, where modern clients frequently stipulate that decorative work be done in this proven medium. Today, decorative painters like to display a carton of broken eggshells in the work setting, as an indication that they work in this technique, but some admit that in a tight corner, working against time, they substitute modern acrylic colours, gouache, or whatever comes to hand and dries most rapidly.

Oil paints – pigments bound with a variety of volatile oils, including linseed oil – were in common use in Scandinavia by the seventeenth century. Although oil paints were considered expensive, their use spread rapidly as painters at every level discovered their advantages. Decorative painters exploited all the properties of oil paint that fine artists had already utilized: richer colours, a flexibility that allowed the paint to be applied thickly, or spread finely as a glaze – so permitting new subtleties of modelling – and a new succulence of texture. The fact that it could be blended and 'softened' made it ideal for marbling and graining techniques. At the same time, oil-based paints started to be used as a general covering when painters found how well they performed as a finish for internal joinery, and furniture. Oil paint dried more slowly than distemper, but faster than egg tempera, and gave a tough surface with a handsome sheen that enriched the dark colours popular during the period. For economy's sake it was usually used in combination with cheap distemper, the latter applied to the walls above dado level, and to ceilings, while the oil paint was used elsewhere. In peasant homes oil paint was rarely used anywhere but on painted furniture before the nineteenth century.

Until the middle of the nineteenth century painters made their own oil paint, combining pigment, which had first to be finely pulverized with a muller and ledger (both of a hard close-grained stone) with the oil. Towards the end of the nineteenth century, chemists began to supply pigments already mixed in oil, to which painters needed only to add turpentine and/or more oil as required. This saved a great deal of laborious grinding and mixing, and gave more reliable results, but experts believe that the impurities and irregular particles of hand-ground pigment gave the earlier, less-refined paints a liveliness of colour and texture that disappeared when the grinding process was mechanized.

The basic white oil paint was made with white lead or chalk, until zinc white was formulated in the mid-nineteenth century. Apart from the dangers of handling lead, generally known by the eighteenth century, mixing white lead with oil was backbreaking work, because of the sheer weight of the pigment. Chalk becomes transparent in oil, so it was chiefly used to give body to the mixture and extend the pigments. In this century titanium white replaced most of the other white base pigments.

A modern recipe for white linseed-oil paint, based on traditional precedents, used by Norwegian conservationists is given below.

For 1 litre of paint mix together:
0.7 kg boiled linseed oil
0.2 kg titanium white powdered pigment
1.0 kg zinc white powder pigment

Subdued colours, nibbled textures, and an unself-conscious medley of objects from different periods, stamp this corner of an expanded stuga as unmistakably Scandinavian, indeed Swedish. While the stove and stencilled wall decoration are early nineteenth century, and the awkward tripod table probably later, the long-case clock is older, and the battered wall cupboard, whose paint has long since worn away, seems to hark back to the seventeenth century. The small box standing next to the stove was almost certainly made to hold the family's store of candles, and would formerly have been hung from the wall.

Driers are added to this mixture in the proportion of 2–5% of the total paint weight. This gives a drying time of between 12–24 hours.

To make a basic paste that can serve as undercoat, middle coat and top coat, depending how much thinner is added, a little linseed oil is tipped into a small pail. The pigments above are added, and stirred and crushed with something like a pestle to get a smooth paste. An electric beater can be used at this stage, but a word of warning: electric gadgets should not be used once white spirit thinner is added because there is a risk of explosion.

The idea behind the successive coats is that one moves from 'lean' (or less oil) to 'fat' (more oil); this gives greatest bonding between coats, plus maximum flexibility and waterproofing in the top coat. A traditional paint like this dries with a subdued sheen, less shiny than a commercial eggshell finish.

Different proportions of oil and white spirit are used to make up the different grades: for the undercoat, the basic mixture is thinned with a half-and-half mixture of linseed oil and white spirit; the mid-coat is diluted with a mixture of two-thirds oil to one-third white spirit and the top coat is made by diluting the base mixture with linseed oil only.

To make pale colours, dry colour can be added to the basic paste, first mixed with linseed oil. The paste can be whisked electrically, but it should be added to the mid-coat by hand because of the white spirit content. It is not needed in the priming coat, and may be whisked into the top coat.

To make dark colours, pigment should be used in making the initial paste and added before the titanium and zinc powder, which is mixed in gradually to lighten the colour. The presence of even a small amount of white alters a dark shade dramatically. To darken colours, an umber pigment especially raw umber, is better than black because it gives subtler shades (unobtainable commercially) and because black has a tendency to make paint lumpy.

Scandinavian furniture was made from good-quality softwood and the joinery was of a high standard, so the minimum of filling – using linseed oil putty – was needed. Mostly the paint was applied directly to the wood in successive coats, moving from 'lean' to 'fat' as already described. It was applied in thin coats, which were well brushed out. In earlier times the first priming coat had its own colour, distinct from what was to go on top. The colour chosen was cheap, relatively opaque and fast drying. Anyone wishing to restore, or imitate Scandinavian period decoration will find that using the correct under-colour helps the final effect to look convincing. There were many variations, but common colours used were blue-black (made from lamp black) up until 1800, light grey (made of lead white and lamp black) until the mid-nineteenth century and yellow ochre from then until the present.

A detail of the scene shown opposite, this is a good illustration of some of the different paint textures in common use in Scandinavia until this century. The clock, with its baroque-style swags, would have been painted with linseed oil paint, probably lead white and Prussian blue, the greenish cast being due to yellowing of linseed oil over the years. The walls, with their stencilled scheme in black and white on pink, are all distempered.

ABOVE *Almost every surface in this picture, even the pottery, has been painted and decorated. The stencilled wall pattern was inspired by an early nineteenth-century wallpaper, but it has a real affinity with the patterned border of some of the family's treasured ceramic plates. The wall shelves are painted brown-red, probably to suggest mahogany. The implements hanging on the left, also painted at one time, were used in beating out flax to make linen.*

ABOVE *There is a lot of painted furniture in Scandinavia with the rather appealingly worn and battered look of these three tiny chairs in Karlstad, which were clearly made for toddlers to sit on, and would once have been painted white, or creamy white, using linseed oil paint. The wildly marbled dado behind is a good example of the bold style of marbling which was characteristic of provincial painters working with distemper paint.*

LEFT *The superb texture and colour of old surfaces painted the traditional way, with many thin coats of linseed oil paint directly onto bare wood without undercoat or primer, show up well in this handsome pair of doorways in an old farmhouse at Skansen. A similar shade of blue, but in distemper, was used as a base for stenkmålning (spattering) in black and white, below the dado. The 'hearty peasant patterns' beloved of Carl Larsson are unusually vivid with their splashes of vermilion red.*

Traditionally made and applied oil paint was meant to last for decades and more, and surviving examples prove just how well the paint has worn. In painted furniture, especially, it often seems to have improved with age: not chipping, flaking or coming apart as modern paints rapidly do, but simply rubbing away gradually over areas of greatest wear. Where chalk was used in the paint, it has tended to become more transparent with time, and the underlying grain of the painted wood shows through delicately, with a suggestion of texture.

These then were the standard types of paint used for most purposes in Scandinavia up to the twentieth century, at least where a good professional finish was required. Undoubtedly, the basic ingredients varied from time to time, place to place, and painter to painter. However, anyone who has seen a fair amount of Scandinavian decorative painting, both in interiors and on furniture, receives the impression that there is such a thing as a Scandinavian 'palette', that certain colours or tones and certain colour combinations are recognizable as characteristic. A number of typical Scandinavian colours were derived from naturally occurring minerals or industrial by-products. The range includes the ochres, umbers, green earth, and Kassell brown. The Swedish and Norwegian ironworks, for example, provided a ready source of iron oxide, and the iron-oxide colours, from the familiar red-brown confusingly known in Scandinavia as English Red, through yellow-browns to the purple-brown-red known as *caput mortuum*, found a prominent and permanent place in the Scandinavian colour range. English Red was widely used in the post-Renaissance period as a background to grisaille, and it is probably the single most popular colour for rustic painted furniture throughout Scandinavia.

The first period in which it is possible to recognize a distinctive Scandinavian painted style is in the seventeenth century. A deep blue-black, relieved by English Red or cinnabar red (more aristocratic), some marbling, grisaille and a great deal of gold leaf, is a commandingly handsome and popular colour scheme at this period, and one that can be found in palaces, castles, and manors, and even in small farmhouses, though without the gilding in the latter. In combination with either a scrubbed bare floor, or the black-and-white painted chequers known as a 'picture floor' because the inspiration for them came from Dutch paintings, this adds up to one of the most satisfactory of all Scandinavian colour schemes to a modern eye.

The early eighteenth century saw the spread of the European fashion for the rococo to Scandinavia, introducing a lighter, prettier palette, as Andreas Lindblom has pointed out: 'pink, mid-blue, apple green, straw yellow, and above all *perl grott* or pearl grey. Gilding is restricted to mouldings and ornament. White is never used, and marbling sparingly. Pleasure and cheerfulness animate this decorative style.'

The French-influenced colours that Scandinavia adopted as its own, and still uses, included pearl grey, mid-blue and straw yellow, all of which frequently appear on fine painted furniture of the period, as well as in some surviving interiors. Stronger colours returned to fashion towards the end of the eighteenth century, and a predilection for forceful colour contrasts developed steadily until one finds illustrations of

Painted and decorated in what have come to seem the typical Scandinavian baroque colours, deep blues and greens with touches of red. This suite of rooms from the small Finnish manor of Lebbellska gården, retains its colourful painted ceiling, an interestingly marbled door, as well as a fine collection of furniture and bibelots, plain wood as well as painted. Note the massive legs on the painted bureau on the left. Also the splendid model sailing ship under the window.

33

the Empire period showing startling juxtapositions of grey and sap green, yellow ochre and dark blue, maroon and grey-green.

The modern Scandinavian practice of painting all the woodwork in a room in one uniform colour, usually an undemanding white, cream or pale grey, was not found at this period. Window-frames and ceilings were commonly white, to maximize light. However, skirtings were often painted a dark (practical) colour, and doors in yet another, unless they were grained to imitate expensive imported hardwoods such as Cuban mahogany. By the mid-nineteenth century the palette had softened again, warm pastels with a greyish cast being especially popular. *Gammel rosa*, or old pink, was a favourite and fashionable decorating shade, made by tinting white paint or distemper with English Red and lamp black. Appearing grey in natural light, it becomes rosy under artificial light, thus giving two favourite colours in one.

Aniline colours were introduced in the middle of the century and were used first for textiles and then for wallpapers. The colour combinations were somewhat lurid and they inevitably influenced decoration and paint colours generally. Uneasy colour marriages, such as raspberry pink and ochre yellow, purple and mustard, royal blue and chrome yellow, were used, though there was also a penchant for the sort of plush and chenille colours – maroon, brown, dark green – that we tend to think of as Victorian. To judge from the carefully preserved studies of Henrik Ibsen and August Strindberg, sombreness of colour, unhappily allied to fussy and garish manufactured furnishings, became the norm in even relatively progressive bourgeois circles.

Spattering with white distemper and birch twigs over English red produces the highly effective wall finish shown here, contrasted with strong blue for woodwork and dado. The doors have been painted in the same brown red. Note the very simple trompe-l'oeil *border, with its stars and triangles.*

Peasant art, however, had meantime enjoyed a most fertile and flourishing period, the newly accessible colours, decorating ideas and furnishings coming together in a triumphantly colourful swan song for the Scandinavian peasant tradition. The peasant cottages that Carl Larsson admired and painted, and to some extent imitated in his own Lilla Hyttnas, were more comfortable, better furnished and more lavishly and imaginatively painted than they had ever been. Many of the most intensely decorated painted interiors date from around the middle of the century; red walls are stencilled or spattered in white, green-painted walls and furniture bloom like a flower garden with the elaborate surface colour effects known as *rosmålning*, farmer marbling puts in a dramatic appearance, spatter painting is commonplace. Some peasant cottages have rooms painted in a rather murky version of *tapeter*, with pilasters, religious scenes and marbling, covered with a heavy varnish.

Although reflecting, at some distance in time, changing taste in the fashionable world, the peasantry stuck to the colours they had always liked and used for their furniture and decoration. Many shades of blue were used, from a gay rococo sky blue popular in Skåne, to the dark thundery blue black used in Hålsingland. English Red, cheap and cheerful, was widely popular, but interesting chestnut-to-maroon colours (based on *caput mortuum*) were much used on built-in furniture. Green seems to have been more popular in Norway, grey in Sweden. Furniture colours tended to be darker and stronger than wall colours. Furniture painters were by now making use of tinted glazes as a final attention to decorated pieces, where it blended decoration and background colours together harmoniously. One might argue that such sophisticated techniques coincided with the onset of decline. By the end of the nineteenth century the countryside was becoming depopulated by substantial waves of emigration to North America and by a general drift to urban centres. As the artistic movement called National Romanticism sang the praises of the rural culture of Scandinavia, the dogged energies and deep pride which had been its mainspring were transferring themselves elsewhere.

Any attempt to regenerate rural culture an age of television, cars, refrigerators and so forth, can only be self-conscious. With the honourable exception of some latter-day *rosmaling*, most recent products offered as peasant or rustic work, like the Dalarna horses (little wooden horses painted red or blue) have a mass-produced air about them. However, an astonishing legacy of rural art remains, tucked away in villages, remote cottages and deserted farms. Modern Scandinavia is sufficiently distanced from its peasant past to begin to want to rediscover it and preserve it. Younger people think about restoring the peasant cottages they buy as summer homes, as well as modernizing them. Scandinavian decoration has been a long time sloughing off the chilly legacy of the Modern Movement. Decorative essays are still timid, and a little spatter painting and a diminutive stencilled border is enough for most people. But with so much wonderfully lusty and colourful peasant work of the last two centuries still there to inspire, the signs are that a more vigorous and adventurous use of painted decoration and traditional colour schemes, re-interpreting the past rather than prolonging it, is just around the corner.

THE SCANDINAVIAN PALETTE

The swatches illustrated here are a selection of some of the key colours used in Scandinavian painting on wood. On the whole the paler shades would have been used for more refined furniture, and the stronger colours on more rustic pieces, with or without further coloured decoration, but this is by no means an invariable rule. Some peasant pieces, especially from the southern Swedish province of Skane, were typically painted in a light sunny blue similar to the one shown here, while some fine pieces such as the eighteenth-century bureau shown on page 105 were sometimes finished in one of the stronger 'rustic' colours to emphasize their Scandinavian provenance.

Blues, greens, greys and straw yellows are used on painted furniture everywhere, but nonetheless, the particular shades illustrated have a distinctively Scandinavian 'feel'; the blues are intense, the greens mellow, the yellows cool and mild like young barley. The greys are warm, the red gentle but substantial. It is important to remember that these colours as shown are 'raw material' in the sense that they have neither been overglazed nor varnished, both processes which considerably modify any given paint shade. Most historic painted pieces will either have been finished with a tinted overglaze to blend and soften the overall effect, or been varnished as protection, the resulting varnished colour gradually yellowing and darkening over the years. In this respect blues, for instance, acquire a noticeably greenish cast.

But what distinguishes Scandinavian paintwork is not so much the colours used, as the extremely subtle texture arrived at by using intense, matt, semi-transparent colour directly over bare wood, so that both the grain and the natural wood colour are faintly discernible.

This is clearly shown in the painted wood colour swatches. The effect of the underlying wood colour and grain is most conspicuous with the pale colours, which are warmed and enlivened, but on any large painted piece in one of the darker colours a woodiness makes itself felt, quite subtly, but distinctly, contributing an extra and very appealing dimension to the whole.

Scandinavia could hardly lay claim to a monopoly of linseed oil and turpentine paint, but its use directly over bare wood, without filling or undercoating of any sort, does appear to be a special and characteristic development. This arises, as may easily be imagined, on the excellent quality of both native timber and joinery in the

Scandinavian countries. Historically, whatever timber was used in furniture making, softwoods such as pine, fir, or soft hardwood such as birch were well grown, free of knots, and well seasoned. Filling was scarcely needed. Only linseed-oil putty, which has a certain elasticity, was ever used to fill the better furniture. Whereas paint was often used in other parts of Europe – Italy for instance – to mask and ennoble inferior materials, Scandinavian painters were free to exploit the qualities of the underlying material. This makes for an honesty of approach and delicacy of effect that definitely contribute to the impression of noble sturdiness which one retains from looking at a wide range of traditionally painted Scandinavian furniture.

All the colour samples shown have been painted with the traditional paint recipe favoured in Scandinavia until the advent of modern alternatives fifty or so years ago. The formula is extremely simple: 50 per cent each of linseed oil and turpentine (white spirit or other turpentine substitutes are allowable today, but increasingly frowned upon in health-conscious painters' unions in Scandinavia due to their suspected harmful effects) coloured with dry pigments, which are easily available in Scandinavia. Dry pigments are as pure as can be, which gives colours mixed with them a vibrant clarity. To make up a paint of this sort, the dry pigment should be mixed with turpentine to a thick cream, to which oil is added gradually, stirring and blending. A very little terebine drier – 2 or 3 drops to a pint of paint – is added to speed the drying time. Compared with a modern commercial paint, this makes a paint which is thin and fluid, without the 'body' of paints designed to cover and obliterate in the least possible number of coats. The first application does not make a striking colour change; many coats, depending on the colour required, may be needed to reach the desired intensity of colour. Cheap and pleasing it may be, but this is not a 'convenience' paint in our sense of the word. On the other hand, once the desired finish is arrived at, there is a considerable satisfaction in knowing that this apparently primitive formula will tend to improve with time and use, eroding away inimitably on the handled surfaces, darkening and mellowing a little, but all the while developing a patina to do with oxidation, wear, gradual hardening and desiccation – a process which is as complex and elusive as the powdery bloom on old marble or the vivid blue-green patination which is such a beautiful adventitious ornament to public statuary in any Scandinavian city.

Contemporary restorers of old painted furniture, or woodwork, are obliged to use this antique paint if their intervention is to be sympathetic to the original. But there is a clear message here for anyone wishing to make something special of an old piece of pine furniture, perhaps stripped during the craze for 'honey coloured pine' during the 1960s and 1970s. Any decently made piece made with straight grained pine acquires the most sympathetic possible glorification, flattering but unpretentious, treated to several coats of this simple old paint tinted with one of the traditional colour formulas, tried and tested over several centuries, given below.

Paint formulas for a range of Scandinavian colours are given below. The proportions are not precise, and it is advisable – as well as enjoyable – to practise and experiment on fillets of wood.

White with 5 per cent oxide red

White with 10 per cent black,
5 per cent oxide red

Chartreuse yellow with 10 per cent white,
2 per cent white

Chartreuse yellow with 50 per cent white

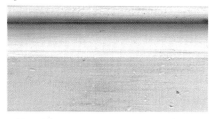

White with 10 per cent raw (green) umber

White with 10 per cent Prussian blue,
5 per cent black

White with 20 per cent cerulean blue

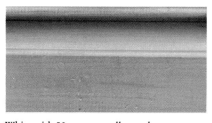

White with 50 per cent yellow ochre

Dala blue with 16 per cent white

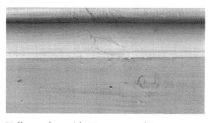

Yellow ochre with 50 per cent white

Mars orange with 10 per cent black

White with 20 per cent Prussian blue,
10 per cent black

White with 2 per cent black

Variations on traditional colours

These colour swatches illustrated here show how the basic colour formulas can be modified, either by adding a little white or black to the mixed up paint, or by overglazing with a half-and-half mixture of oil and turpentine tinted with just enough colour to make a visible difference when the mixture is brushed out over the dried oil paint surface. Overglazing was commonly used as a finishing process on decoratively painted furniture, grand or provincial, to soften colours, blend applied decoration into the background colour, and give a flatering patina to the whole piece. The choice of tinting colour for the overglaze depended on the effect required; to merely soften and age a brightly decorated painted piece, murky tints – raw umber, burnt umber, or black, or a combination of these – were used, swabbed over the entire surface with a soft cloth and then rubbed down with a clean cloth, or the palm of the hand, till the piece looked right. There are no rules for this type of finish, the painter's own tastes decide whether overglazing is a mere film, or casts a noticeable shadow. Because the dark pigment lodges in any unevennesses in the previous paint surfaces, it gives a pleasantly distressed effect almost effortlessly.

Tinting the overglaze with a colour related to one of the colours used in the decoration of the piece opens up other possibilities which were similarly exploited by Scandina-

| Mixed with black over white base | Mixed with white over white base | Colour alone over white base | Colour over dark base wood | Colour over light base wood |

Raw sienna

Yellow ochre

Vandyke brown

Caput mortuum

vian painters. *Rosmålning* painters, for instance, often overglazed a brightly decorated piece with a glaze tinted with the background colour of the piece, green, blue, chestnut or whatever, which had the effect of softening violent colour contrasts and unifying the overall effect without 'dirtying' the colour scheme. This idea could be developed further, of course, by overglazing with a subtly different colour from the base colour: blue on green, say, or drab green on red. Again there are no rules; experiment, and the look of the piece in question, will dictate the best procedure. The appeal of overglazing in this way was and is (it is still an important part of decorative painting) that it offers a quick last-minute means of correcting, modifying or enhancing a completed decorative scheme. The degree of added colour is easily controlled during the rubbing-back stage. Usually a little more colour was left around carving or mouldings, to emphasize them, while projections such as leading edges of cornices might be wiped almost clean. Not all the traditional painted furniture would have been varnished as a final protection. Varnishes were not really necessary for overglazed linseed-oil paint and would have tended to add too much gloss to a paint system with its own subdued texture.

A selection of authenticated traditional Scandinavian eighteenth-century oil paint colours.

Mixed with black over white base	Mixed with white over white base	Colour alone over white base	Colour over dark base wood	Colour over light base wood

English Red (Engelsk Rott)

Burnt Sienna

Cobalt Blue

Green Earth

PAINTERS AND CLIENTS

Considering the scale of their contribution to Scandinavian architecture and interiors at every social level, decorative painters have remained largely unsung heroes, their names in all but a few instances either unknown or forgotten, and their professional history and methods of work scantily documented. But, then, little mystique or special status attached to artists of any kind before the Renaissance. Painting was regarded as a trade plied by largely anonymous craftsmen. During the Renaissance secular panel paintings, for display in private houses, became fashionable and a new market for paintings, distinct from church patronage, appeared. At the same time the skill of the artist became an important consideration and individual reputations began to emerge.

In Scandinavia, painted colour had been used as decoration for carvings and rune stones since at least the days of the Vikings, but the first clients for decorative painting on a large scale were the proselytizing bishops and clergy of the newly established Christian church. They must have realized early on that painting could play an important role as propaganda in the new churches being built all over Scandinavia. It was a means of dramatizing the Old and New Testament stories and as a (relatively) economical way of adding splendour to the interiors of the quite modest, often vernacular-style, church buildings.

A lavishly decorated interior like this one from Skansen open-air museum, in Stockholm, represents prosperous peasant tastes of the early nineteenth century. Blue is much in evidence, but warmed by exceptionally handsome marbling on the built-in bed and pretty stencilled decoration, imitating wallpaper, above the dado. The long-case clock is from Mora, the region celebrated for its clock making, and was always meant to be read *as a sign of affluence as well as a useful timepiece. The bed is – literally – a cupboard bed in the sense that a tall closet has been grafted on to the end facing out into the room, marbled en suite with the heavy cornice to give something of the air of a four-poster. Most built-in beds are more crudely constructed than this one. The whitewashed ceiling was intended to reflect more light.*

The first church painter of whom we know more than his name is the Swede, Albertus Pictor (1440–1509) – to use the latinized version of his name found in church records. Born and raised in Stockholm, which meant that he was exposed to what was most advanced in artistic trends in Sweden in his day, Albert the Painter combined considerable artistic talent with an entrepreneurial flair and capacity for hard work that made him a rich man. He owned three stone houses in Stockholm, which represented a great fortune for a self-made man in a country where stone buildings were the exception and usually lived in by the nobility. As well as his church painting, he ran an embroidery workshop specializing in sewing pearls on to church vestments and a cassock of his design is still in the possession of Uppsala Cathedral. There are clear similarities between ornament used in painted decoration and in embroidery during the Middle Ages.

In the intervals of completing decorative schemes for parish churches, painters were often employed on similar projects in the castles and homes of the local nobility and gentry. There is a close and continuous relationship in Scandinavia between decorative work in churches and aristocratic homes, which becomes most pronounced in the so-called 'Scandinavian Baroque' period of the seventeenth century; church interiors of that time resemble state rooms in noble castles and mansions.

Though much faded, this detail of a wall by the font at Tierps church is interesting because it clearly shows stencils used to create a powdering of motifs across a frieze of figures, now barely visible. More stencils would have been used for the cross-ways band. The stylized painted drapery is an interesting feature.

Albertus Pictor was the best-known, as well as most prosperous, church painter of the late medieval period, and much of his decorative work survives to this day, though in varying states of repair. This intensely decorated vault is at Hårkeberga church, north of Stockholm, and depicts scenes from the life of Christ with a cluster of apocalyptic beasts at the apex. At this time, church paintings were done in water-based paints, either tinted limewash or distemper, which accounts for the delicate translucency of the colours even where, as here, they have faded with time. Bands of pattern, as on the ribs of the vault, are a feature of the painter's style. He is known to have used stencils for repeat patterning to cover the ground more quickly, and it is possible that the bold repeats on the ribs are stencilled.

ABOVE *Deep rich colours, offset by gilding, were one of the characteristic features of church decoration during the Scandinavian baroque period, giving a solid, secular bourgeois feel in contrast to the polychrome fantasias of earlier centuries. Blue was the prime favourite colour, though dark drab-green and chestnut browns were also popular. These strong schemes were lightened as a rule by passages of marbling, usually based on the main colour used. The painted drapery here is in a more realistic and* trompe-l'oeil *manner than in the Renaissance style swagging shown on page 42.*

RIGHT *The three wise men are paying homage to the Christ child in this touching and delicate vignette from Hårkeberga Kyrka. The Star of Bethlehem hovers above the stable, and the Virgin wears a flowering robe of gorgeous pattern and medieval style, high-waisted and with flowing sleeves. Fronds decorating the wall to the right of the picture are another feature of the style of Albertus Pictor. By comparing this with photos of eighteenth-century painted ceilings at Hembygsgården, with their very similar feathery decoration, it is possible to gauge the persistence of ornamental motifs in the Scandinavian vernacular culture. The later fronds are more elaborate, and formally organized, but there is a clear line of descent between the sixteenth-century decoration and its eighteenth-century successor. Note the colourful and eccentric marbling on the pew to the right.*

A magnificent grisaille and trompe-l'oeil ceiling in the grand Scandinavian manner from Tidö castle in Sweden. The intention of this style of seventeenth-century ceiling decoration was to imitate the highly decorated stucco ceilings then fashionable in the great houses of Europe. As often happened with Scandinavian borrowings of this sort, the faux stucco ceiling ended up as a triumphantly decorative invention in its own right. A ceiling of this scale would almost certainly have been painted on canvas before being fixed in place, but many smaller versions were painted in situ, sometimes across boarded ceilings, cracks and all. The most handsome grisaille ceilings, like the one shown here, or the ceiling at Läckö (page 129) are picked out in a contrast colour, usually red. The glimpse of painted sky in the middle is an unusual touch.

Painters who worked for the wealthiest noble families, and especially for the Royal family, invariably included a few foreigners, imported for their skill in reproducing fashionable European ideas. As time went on their local apprentices moved off to undertake work of their own, and fashionable ideas, colours and techniques began to percolate down the social scale, so that the 'best room' of a prosperous but modest farmstead often repeats, more crudely, and on a smaller scale, effects seen and admired in grander settings. By the time such ideas reached the peasant artist, they had often become garbled in travelling so far from their source.

At first glance it is hard to trace a connection between this painted ceiling rosette (RIGHT) from a wooden cottage and the grandiose example in grisaille shown below. Nevertheless the derivation is incontestable, the aristocratic idea moving gradually down through the social classes and becoming almost unrecognizable – though still decorative along the way.

ABOVE *Painted decoration of quite exceptional finesse, from a slightly later date than Sturehov, is shown in this detail of painted wall-hangings at Bjorkssund together with a particularly felicitous painted treatment, imitating flowered striped silk, on the charming bedhead. All the stripes on the panel, as well as the trompe mouldings, are hand painted.*

OPPOSITE *By the latter half of the eighteenth century Scandinavian decorative painters were well up to European standards of elegance and techniques as this picture of a lavishly pretty interior from Sturehov manor demonstrates convincingly. It is the work of Lars Bolander, whose earlier work in the same sprightly rococo style can be seen at Ekolssund, also not far from Stockholm.*

By the early years of the eighteenth century, rich patrons were beginning to see the wisdom of sending talented young artists to study in Europe for a few years, before setting them up as Master Painters on their return. This may have been prompted by the difficulties experienced by the architect Nicodemus Tessin the Younger (son of the immigrant architect Nicodemus the Elder) in recruiting skilled foreign painters to decorate the new Royal Palace in Stockholm. At all events two of the painters who were to dominate Swedish art during the eighteenth century, Jean Erik Rehn and Johann Pasch, spent several years studying and training in Europe before returning to work in Sweden, where they were almost immediately recruited to help with interiors in the Royal Palace. With 600 rooms this is the world's largest royal residence, which may explain why it took so long to build (*c.* 1700–1754), and why so many different artists were recruited over the years.

Three of the painters recruited by Nicodemus Tessin and his project architect, Carl Hårleman, in Paris, were so dismayed by the uncouthness and provincialism of decorative painting as practised in Sweden that they started up a school, and taught evening classes themselves in order to train local painters. This eventually became the Konstakadamien or Academy of Art. It could well be that the expert technique and sophisticated style of later Swedish decorative painters such as Lars Bolander, who painted rooms at Ekolssund and Sturehov, owed something to a course of evening classes at this school. Certainly decorative painting in aristocratic houses in Sweden and Denmark from this period onwards is noticeably more refined and elegant. At the same time it loses the gusto and boldness which seems to bring earlier, cruder decorative work bouncing off the walls.

The finest decorative work is often the result of a fruitful collaboration between an imaginative patron and a talented artist. The witty and charming *trompe-l'oeil* at Åkerö painted by Johan Pasch for Carl Gustav Tessin is one striking example. Intended for the private cabinet of this worldly Francophile, who had spent many years as Swedish ambassador at Versailles, the little room exhibits a playfulness and imagination rare in upper-class Scandinavian interiors. Brilliantly life-like and convincing *trompe-l'oeil* alcoves contain Tessin's personal possessions: musical instruments, books, and a lap dog that seems about to topple out of its niche onto the floor. The care and affection with which this portrait *in absentia* (of the client) was painted suggest an unusually warm rapport between the artist and Tessin himself.

Gustav III (1746–1792) with his formidable intelligence and fastidious taste greatly influenced the decorative arts of Sweden. Like Britain's Prince Regent, or that other extravagant Royal, Marie-Antoinette, Gustav had enough prestige and confidence to impose his taste forcefully on the arts, and give them a new direction. Brilliantly talented, cultivated and cosmopolitan, Gustav was a true monarch of the Enlightenment. Under his guidance and patronage, a style of decoration and furnishing emerged that, although deriving inspiration chiefly from European neo-classicism, became authentically Swedish. Proof of the integrity of the Gustavian style is that its essential charm and refinement survived imitation at the hands of countless provincial furniture makers and painters, of middle-class housewives draping

ABOVE *The mysterious subaqueous green used to paint the walls of this little manor-house parlour may have been tinted with arsenic. Faux 'panel' work at its simplest, merely rectangles of simulated moulding, lends a touch of formality echoed by a fine gilt looking-glass and elegant cabriole legs on the painted table. The stylized drapery above the window is still seen all over Scandinavia, sometimes teamed with slender muslin curtains. This is a quintessentially Scandinavian interior.*

ABOVE *The focus of painted decoration in this room in Hälsingland is undoubtedly the door, strikingly decorated in the regional style known as 'clouds' marbling, in characteristic blues and blacks with floral panels inset. Harder to see, because the distemper colours have faded so much, is the delicate rococo decoration of the walls, with flower sprays contained within a rocaille frame.*

RIGHT *The simple effectiveness of the 'clouds' formula shows up clearly in this detail of the door above. An adept painter would have painted the arabesque 'cloud' shapes with two colours on one straight-cut brush, light blue on two-thirds of the bristles and white on the rest – a trick used to exploit the wider range of tones that results in expert hands.*

their windows with neo-classical muslin, even of the twentieth-century manufacturers of reproduction Gustavian furniture by the container load.

While the court painters, and master painters such as Pasch, Rehn and Bolander, were making reputations for themselves by working in the private palaces of the rich and powerful, the painters whose skills brought excitement and colour to the homes of lesser people – squires, yeomen farmers, the better-off peasants – lived in the same unremarked obscurity as those ancestors of theirs who had put so much of themselves into the decoration of the medieval painted churches. Some individual names have been handed down; these are usually those of painters who worked in a wide range of venues, painting furniture for peasant homes, or canvas *tapeter* for manor houses and church interiors. These painters would have ranged the countryside in the summer with samples, looking for commissions to occupy themselves with during the winter. Sometimes they might stop in one place for a while if a commission to redecorate a room came up. They were paid either with money, or more often in kind with a fat piglet, a goose or a bushel of corn, which they would pick up on the return journey, towards the end of summer.

Examples of *kurbits* painting found in regions far from its native Dalarna are known to have been painted by roving Dalarnian painters. Some of the painters of these elaborate scenes of flowers and figures are known by name. The leading exponent of the *kurbits* school, was Malar Erik Eliasson from Rattvik who worked around the turn of the nineteenth century. The villages of Leksand and Rattvik in Dalarna both acquired reputations in their day for the quality and skill of their native *kurbits* painters.

Other peasant styles whose practitioners are known by name are the wild wood-graining combined with floral decoration found in Vasterbotten towards the middle of the nineteenth century. Two painters, Marten Linstrom and Johan Fredrik Lundgren, are known to have used this style. Peasant marblers, who began with church marbling and took their work into farms and cottages in southern Sweden, include Torsten Wennerberg and Kristoffer Fisher, whose church work is documented. One of the most striking individual decorative styles in furniture painting, a combination of blue, black and white marbling with painted floral panels, was the invention of Johan Backstrom who had, unusually for a peasant painter, some academic training. He worked mainly in south-eastern Sweden.

This photograph vividly evokes the sheer spread of painted effects in a more prosperous peasant interior. Aside from the floor, left bare as usual, every surface (with the sole exception of a chair in the foreground), has been decorated, from the figure of party 'bouncer'

Knut by the doorway of the party room (the work of Corporal Gustav Reuter), to the favourite white-on-red spatter finish on the wall of the furthest room, not forgetting a rustic grisaille rosette in the middle. It is not likely that all this colourful work was done en suite, at one go: more

likely it was added to gradually and piecemeal, a room at a time, over many years. We know, for instance, that seventeen years elapsed between the start of Reuter's wall-painting in the party room and its completion.

Names are reassuring, but it is the paintings which tell us about the men who painted them, and by extension, about the peasant societies in which they lived. Painters often included written inscriptions on painted furniture decoration and wall paintings. These might be proverbial sayings, sentimental allusions to family events or Biblical quotations. There is even the odd smutty joke. Now and then these inscriptions are highly critical of the client, complaining of their stinginess or the poor food dished out. One can only assume that their customers were illiterate; otherwise the painter's jocular revenge must have backfired unpleasantly. 'Talking pictures' were popular with peasant clients. These were portraits in a caricature style with suitable remarks written beside the faces; 'I would like to be married soon' by a portrait of a pretty young woman explains itself, and there is sometimes a satiric element as in the picture that accompanies the bland self-introduction 'I am a grocer'. Another talking picture of a traditional sort, invariably painted by the doorway into a best or feast room, which was often added on to cottages in southern Sweden, shows a man in a threatening posture, usually brandishing a stick or a sword. In the Hålsingland farmhouse at Skansen Museum, the man wears a frock coat and a wide-brimmed hat and carries a pitchfork. 'My name is Knut, and if anyone misbehaves I will throw him out', runs the written inscription; a warning to guests not to overstep the quite generous limits to acceptable behaviour.

Not spattered but stencilled in a striking lacy pattern apparently modelled on damask or brocade, white-on-red distemper creates an effect buoyant enough to stand up to three feet of snow outside.

It was usual, though not invariable, to choose religious themes for the decoration of party or festive rooms like the one shown here from Skansen. More often a suitably convivial subject, such as the miracle at Cana where Jesus changed water into wine, was chosen; here, though the floral frames are bright and attractive, the subject is the Crucifixion, giving the window wall something of the solemn air of an altar adorned with a triptych.

This particular talking picture was one of a series painted in the feast room by Corporal Gustav Reuter (1699–1783), one of the most celebrated of the 'soldier painters'. These men cut something of a dash in rural Sweden in the centuries when every rural '*hundred*' or parish was responsible for choosing and maintaining a professional soldier (or a sailor in coastal areas), nominally pledged to give one month's military service a year in exchange for a soldier's cottage with its own small-holding, a new uniform, weapons and other fighting equipment. The post was not a life-tenure as soldiers needed to be reasonably young and fit for active service. A wounded or unfit incumbent was dismissed. But there was nothing to stop these men, in the peaceful intervals when their services were not required, from carrying on a second trade, and this no doubt was what they turned to in retirement. Some were carpenters, other shoemakers or boat builders, and a surprising proportion of these men seem to have taken up painting. Perhaps they

Wall paintings in a restrained version of the kurbits *style, where large bouquets float above spirited renderings of biblical stories in contemporary dress, bring the gayest of colours into a* stuga *chest/guest room presided over by an unusually chunky pull-out bed piled high with coverlets and pillows. The framed print must be a later addition, because wall paintings were too prized in their heyday for anyone to wish to cover them up, even with another picture.*

found it a peaceful contrast from campaigning abroad. Such men travelled more widely than most peasants, and thus came into contact with a wider world that might provide them with a great range of visual references from which to draw as painters. Certainly Corporal Reuter's paintings in the Hålsingland farmhouse, which show a series of Biblical scenes framed in floral cartouches, are richly decorative, with a sophisticated feeling for colour harmonies. Seventeen years elapsed between Reuter's wall paintings and his ceiling decorations. Perhaps he was called up for military service. Or possibly the family who engaged his services took seventeen years to make up their minds about taking the decorations a step further. One thing can be verified; whatever new experiences he may have undergone in the meantime, there is no evidence of it in his ceiling painting, whose colours, flowers and general style is identical to the earlier paintings on the walls.

THE LITTLE RED HOUSE

The nineteenth century was a time when artists and intellectuals throughout Europe, dismayed by the ruthless pace of industrialization, began to rediscover and celebrate the rich heritage of rural, or peasant, culture and traditions. In England this surge of nostalgic sentiment gave us productions as various as William Morris' rush-seated chairs and hand-loomed tapestries, Housman's *Shropshire Lad*, Cecil Sharp's collections of folk songs and country dance tunes. In Scandinavia a similar spirit informed Ibsen's *Peer Gynt*, Hans Andersen's celebrated tales (many of them based on folk tales told to him as a child), the haunting romanticism of paintings like *The Kantele Player* by the Finnish artist Pekka Halonen, or *Girls Dancing* by the Norwegian artist Halfdan Egedius. But perhaps the most beloved expression of the National Romantic Movement, as the Scandinavians call it, is the book of watercolours, *Ett Hem* (At Home), published by the Swedish painter Carl Larsson in 1899. In this he recorded family life in and around Lilla Hytnas, the red wooden cottage or *stuga* that had been a wedding present from Karin Larsson's well-to-do father. If not the most profound art produced by National Romanticism, it was (and still seems to the countless admirers who journey to see the place every year) the freshest, happiest and most appealing evocation of a rural way of life, which had never seemed so golden as when it was in danger of being extinguished by economic stagnation and the drift from country to town. Using his romping, rosy-cheeked children, elfin wife and a large cast of villagers as models, Larsson depicted the highspots of a Swedish domestic year: name-day and St Lucia ceremonies; Christmas feasts with village wives presiding in brightly embroidered traditional costume; crayfish parties in high summer;

Clusters of little red cottages, strung out along an unmade-up road in green valleys set about with forest, are a commonplace sight throughout the northern Swedish provinces. This particular hamlet near Karlstad, in north western Sweden, has changed very little externally in the last century or two, though most of the stugor (cottages) have been modernized internally, to the extent of having electricity, piped water, and central heating. Most of the families who live here have occupied the same cottages for many generations, adding on a storey or a second cottage (for parents, or children) or an outbuilding.

ABOVE *Diagonal grooving is often used on doors, and shutters, as here, to dramatize what is basically a piece of tongue-and-groove construction. Sometimes the geometry is emphasized by the use of two colours, one for the flat surfaces, another in the grooves.*

OPPOSITE *The appositeness of Falun red as an exterior paint in the Swedish landscape is most convincingly shown up against winter snow, as this view of a handsome stretch of barn and outbuildings near Gävle demonstrates. As with so many Scandinavian farms, the buildings here enfold a central yard to create what is something of a micro-climate in fierce winter weather, shielded from the force of the wind and snow storms, observable from the windows of the main house, a tight little agricultural community embracing rather than standing aloof from the daily activities of the farm.*

family breakfasts *en plein air*; a visit to the carpentry shop, knee-deep in wood shavings; an encounter with an old peasant woman and her heifer; a glimpse of Karin nursing her latest baby. Everyone radiates health and uncomplicated happiness; this is Swedish life with the dark side deliberately left out. 'I want to do good, and cheer, not one person, but everybody!' Larsson had written, many years earlier, and with *Ett Hem*, which was an immediate success, he amply succeeded. But captivating as are the scenes of domestic life, the focal point of *Ett Hem* is the house itself, a rambling wooden gatherum of a cottage, painted outside a glowing Falun red, and inside in the clear colours that form part of the sophisticated folk style that the Larssons seem to have invented. This was as refreshingly novel in its day as Morris' rather different Red House had been to an earlier generation.

Larsson was a gifted, intuitive image-maker. Home is a word with very special resonance to Scandinavians. When the world outside is dark and icy, home needs must be all the more welcoming, bright with 'all those cheery peasant patterns' that Larsson found 'more significant works of art than ... most oil paintings'. There could be no more potent symbol of Scandinavian rural life, with its strong sense of cherished traditions, than the red wooden cottage he paints in so many guises, glimpsed between the filmy green of young birch leaves, embowered in lilac, making a heart-warming splash of colour across a snow-sheeted landscape.

Wooden cottages or cabins – *stuga* can be translated either way – are Scandinavia's most ancient, and have remained the most prevalent, vernacular building. The use of wood needs no explanation in regions where trees are plentiful and easily worked stone is scarce. The ancestor of the *stuga* is a rudimentary Iron Age structure, looking much like an upturned thatched boat. The skeleton consisted of rafters lashed to ridgepieces, which were supported on forked poles braced by cross beams. A central hole in the thatch, which was made from reeds, straw or turves, let out the smoke from an open hearth below. Such dwellings must have been quick to construct. It is interesting to note that in West Jutland fishermen's huts built in the late nineteenth century for the fishing season are constructed in almost exactly the same way, except that they have managed to eliminate the smoke with a chimneystack of sandy turves piled in layers.

In the Iron Age people and livestock lived in the same space, but it is notable that as Scandinavian building methods became more sophisticated, separate spaces were allotted to humans and animals, a nicety unknown in the houses of the Saxons. By Viking times, towards the year 1000, woodcarving and boat-building skills had reached a high level of sophistication. A type of dwelling – the hearth house – had evolved that is recognisably the prototype of the wooden *stuga* found all over northern and western Scandinavia. This was a one-room dwelling for humans only, animals being housed in a separate cabin, sometimes reached via a connecting porch. The walls were made of logs laid horizontally, the underside of each log hollowed to fit over the one beneath, and secured by joints at the corners. The roof-beam, which let into the gables at either end, was covered with tightly set boards to make a shallow pitched roof. The boards were covered with

birch bark, as a form of waterproofing, and over this went either another layer of boards, set horizontally, or a double layer of turves. In winter the shallow pitch of the roof supported a further insulating layer of snow.

Within its limitations, this early form of *stuga*, though still primitive by modern standards, being windowless and chimneyless (the smoke escaped through a vent hole in the roof above a central hearth), was an economical and practical building, for largely forested land with a harsh climate. The log cabin is still a favourite type of building wherever timber is plentiful such as in North America. The construction of a log house may look crude to an uninitiated eye, particularly when the turf-covered roof is shaggy with wild flowers, but it is very well suited to its external environment. It is astonishingly durable providing that it rests on a slightly raised stone foundation, that the logs are weatherproofed externally, especially on the end grain, and

ABOVE *Robust construction offset by almost translucent paintwork, in fine strong colours, is the combination which gives so much rural painted furniture throughout Scandinavia enduring appeal. Until the mid-nineteenth century or so, when new and cheaper pigments unbalanced a native fastidiousness in their use of colour, provincial painters tended to stick with the type of deep, fruity tones shown here.*

RIGHT *This ensemble view of the handsome cupboard detailed above shows how snugly, yet boldly, it inhabits its allotted space in the scheme of things in a* stuga *living space. Pattern on pattern is a fashionable idea which Scandinavian peasants had already taken on board almost two hundred years ago. Scandinavian and other collectors today are apt to stand such numinous pieces as this in blank white settings, for contrast, and out of respect for their intense vitality. But it is immediately obvious how much happier old decorated pieces are in a similarly decorated context, as here, where decorated walls and deep toned paint on the woodwork harmonize with, instead of fighting, the dominant item of furnishing.*

that the roof is carefully maintained. It must have proved its superiority quite quickly over stave construction – where the walls consist of upright posts bedded in the earth – because aside from the churches stave-built structures are a rarity. The major drawback of building with staves was that damp soon entered the buried part of the uprights and rotted them.

With time and increased prosperity, the one-roomed *stuga* expanded to include some extra rooms – a best room, a chest room for storage, even a 'dead body' room for laying out a corpse. But it is clear from carefully preserved early examples (now in museums) that the extra rooms were for show and for occasional use, while the daily activities of family life, cooking, eating, sleeping and working, still took place in one communal room, which was often quite large, and which was now provided with a large open fireplace with a chimneystack, usually set in one corner.

The corner fireplace stamps this as an earlier stuga *interior, predating the introduction of ceramic stoves. This all-purpose hearth cooked food while warming the room. The bright whitewash is recent, but plausible. Such fireplaces were probably whitewashed quite regularly.*

Many such buildings survive from the period (the late seventeenth to the mid-nineteenth centuries) when Scandinavian peasant culture, judging from the vitality and variety of its artefacts, was at its most confident and productive. From the outside, with their weathered or tarred wooden exteriors, they were small and inconspicuous structures of one storey, often surrounded by small satellite buildings used as sheds for animals, wood stores, barns and so forth.

At this time peasant houses were not painted with Falun red, the deep rusty-red exterior paint now found on wooden cottages across Scandinavia, and which – berry-bright against subtly modulated green and grey – seems made to order for the landscape. Its widespread adoption for log houses occurred towards the middle of the nineteenth century, although it was used earlier on grander buildings.

Outwardly then, the peasant cottage was unobtrusively at one with its austere landscape of forest, pasture, rock and water. Only in the south, in Skåne, or across the water, in flat, fertile, village-studded Denmark, was there anything resembling the picturesque cottage of softer climates with a straggle of fruit trees and a neat apron of cottage flowers intermixed with vegetables.

By the eighteenth century, the interior decoration of the *stuga* would probably have consisted of a few prized items of furniture, spectacularly decorated, and of a few vivid textiles, hand embroidered or woven by the women of the family. Inside a *stuga* the first impression is of a dusky woodiness. In Norway and Finland log walls of *gran och tall* – fir and pine – were usual, planed smooth inside, whereas in Sweden planked walls were preferred. Until the end of the seventeenth century most of the furniture was built in. Built-in furniture is a feature of Scandinavian interiors and dates back to the Vikings. Many old cottages have walls honeycombed with cupboard beds, the one nearest the hearth reserved for the very old; sometimes an upper row of smaller alcove beds was supplied for children. The householder and his wife slept in a cupboard bed glorified perhaps by a little carving, or (later on) decorative painting, or by curtains and covers handsome enough to be displayed during the day. Old alcove beds seem painfully small to modern eyes: this was not because Scandinavians were smaller, indeed exceptional height was a national characteristic, but because people slept in a half-sitting position, propped against pillows and covered by feather-filled quilts and fur or sheepskin covers. Delicate sleepers must have suffered torments, as in dormitories everywhere. August Strindberg's sardonic novel, *The People of Hemso*, contains a passage describing the first night passed by the interloping Carlsson in a nineteenth-century peasant home in the archipelago:

'Heavy sighs were heaved, and there was puffing, wheezing and snuffling in the kitchen until snoring was once more at full blast'.

Two beds placed end-to-end across a wall have a small painted cupboard acting as divider between them, just one of the many ingenious ways in which items of furniture were made to serve two purposes at once in the limited space of the traditional all-in-one stuga *living room. In some cottages a whole wall might be taken up by cupboard beds, often with a second tier of tiny sleeping alcoves above, for the children. The beds shown here are not built into the wall, but aspire to the four-poster style, with curtains and pelmets and lace-trimmed valances.*

ABOVE *So much paint is splashed about so generously in traditional cottages that it is salutary to remind oneself that in the beginning was only unadorned wood, the matrix material from which simple necessities of life like these completely honest and functional plates, spoons and containers were fashioned. The sober beauty of such humble domestic items owes everything to the texture of its material honed by daily use.*

OPPOSITE *The sturdy pine table, scrubbed daily, surrounded by bench seating and presided over by the master's chair, is the one invariable item of furniture in peasant cottages, of comparable importance to the fire that was never allowed to go out. Families sat round these long tables to work, as well as eat, and because of this they were always situated next to the window wall, to make the most of daylight.*

It requires no great effort of the imagination to realize that for several generations to live together in one room for much of the year, considerable forbearance, reinforced by iron custom, was needed, and this seems to have been the case in all self-respecting peasant homes. The use of these intensely lived-in spaces was regulated by unwritten rules and customs whose origins must have been lost in antiquity, but which had the force that ancestral wisdom has in rural societies. For instance, a one-room cottage or *morastuga* had a beam suspended from the ceiling (the 'crownrail') that set a boundary beyond which beggars or strangers might not go unless expressly permitted. (It was also, rather confusingly, used for drying clothes.) Womenfolk were accorded the place nearest the fire (not simply from chivalry, but because firelight enabled them to carry on domestic tasks such as spinning and sewing), while the men clustered about the 'seat of honour', reserved for the master of the establishment, which stood at the head of the table on the side of the room furthest from the entrance. There was probably a practical reason for this position as it gave the men of the house time to size up the intentions of unexpected visitors. In spite of the need for caution, an almost sacred importance was attached to hospitality by people in remote valleys, or on unfrequented islets, hungry for news and a new face. In cottages in the northern Swedish province of Hälsingland it was customary to hang a prettily embroidered linen towel by the doorway as a symbol of hospitality.

Sharing food and drink acquired ritual meaning too, through the use of special ceremonial containers, usually made of carved wood in Sweden and Norway, pottery in Denmark, and of birch bark in Finland. Wedding guests, for instance, were expected to take bread, butter, cheese or ale as a gift, and peasants vied with each other in the elaboration of the containers. Perhaps the most familiar of these containers is the *ölgås* or beergoose, a hollow, bird-shaped, wooden goblet which was brought to the feast floating in a great wooden bowl filled with ale. Birthings brought village midwives equipped with fancifully carved wooden porringers with lids, containing the thick barley gruel thought to best sustain nursing mothers.

Apart from the alcove beds, which were shut away behind doors or curtains during the day, the most important furnishings in the *stuga* were a long table of scrubbed pine, around which the family worked and ate. Seating was provided by benches, with the householder occupying the master's chair, which was often the only proper chair, with arms, in the house. Other seating might have included a *kubbstol*, a barrel-shaped chair hollowed from an entire section of tree trunk, or, in forest country where animistic beliefs lingered, one of the odd seats called a *krakstol* contrived from sections of trunk with the legs formed by conveniently placed branches. These have a distinctly trollish appearance, and were believed, in Finland especially, to have magic powers.

Daylight was almost as precious as heat, which is why the sturdy long tables in old cottages tend to be sited close to a window. Candles were a luxury and though rushes, home-made tapers and *crusie*-lamps (a type of oil lamp) gave a little light, the chief light source was always the open fire or (later) stove. The darkest time in the northern Scandinavian winter is usually October just before the snow falls. Snow is a

ABOVE *The freshness of colouring, and decorative élan of this small cupboard are typical of the best provincial work. Even though one knows that such painting was done commercially, and this cupboard was only one among many pieces to be decorated by a particular painter, the exuberance of the colours and the lovingly applied detail convey a sense of joy in the making which is irresistible.*

OPPOSITE *Few small rural houses elsewhere in Europe would be likely to encompass as many painted effects in one corner of a room as can be seen in this detail of an interior at Hembygsgården, in Hålsingland, Sweden. From left to right these are as follows: standard linseed oil paint on the door, stencilled walls in distemper paint above the dado, crude mahogany graining beneath the dado rail, marbling in shades of blue on the chest, and full-blown painted decoration, with Hålsingland 'clouds' marbling on the small wall cupboard. The chair too, might well have been painted at one time. Such a concentration of decorative effects is by no means unusual in the remoter provinces such as Hålsingland, where regional styles of painting flourished inversely, one might suspect, to their distance from major cities.*

powerful reflector, and though the daylight hours are shorter in January, there appears to be more light then because the land is covered in snow. In winter people occupied themselves with small tasks, sitting round the table. Strindberg describes such a scene in *The People of Hemso*:

'Solitude and the snow weighed heavily on their senses and the short hours of daylight permitted only a minimum of work. A fire burned in the stove, the lads were mending the seining-tackle, the girls sat by the spinning-wheel, and Rundqvist was busy carving out spade handles.'

Most Scandinavian peasants would have been competent carpenters as whittling and carving were common ways of passing time. The first item of furniture in peasant homes that was commonly not merely carved, but also decoratively painted, was almost certainly the *kist*, or marriage chest, made by the men of the family for a future bride's linen and clothes. To judge from the loving elaboration shown by the surviving examples found all over Scandinavia, making these was not just a source of pride, but of creative delight. Carved and painted outside and in, chiefly with flower motifs – juicy roses, stiffly towering bouquets – but also with hearts, scrolls, bridal crowns, these eloquently convey the sheer pleasure in making, and joy in handling brilliant colour, which gives Scandinavian peasant painted furniture such a completely different dimension from painted pieces made for the upper classes.

To begin with, painted decoration was reserved for freestanding pieces, like the marriage chests, or a little carved cupboard to hang on the wall. More prosperous peasant families might also have painted wall hangings, like the ones produced by the Dalarnian *kurbits* painters, but these were only brought out to brighten the *stuga* for festivals and other special occasions. But as a wider range of pigments became available, colours spread over more and more surfaces in these dusky wooden interiors, beginning with a freestanding piece, which acquired heirloom status, such as a corner cupboard or wall cupboard, or that special pride of peasant interiors, a painted long-case clock from Mora in Dalarna. Most, though not all, of these items were painted by specialist craftsmen. But there must always have been individuals who discovered a talent for embellishing home-made items for their own family use. Later on, when coloured paint and decoration took the peasant *stuga* by storm – so that bare wood became synonymous with wretched poverty – it is hard to believe that families did not economize by doing a good part of the work themselves.

By the late eighteenth century, colour was widely used throughout the cottage interior, covering built-in furniture and walls – of logs or planks in the north, or of plaster in the southern regions of Scandinavia. The simpler interiors were painted predominantly in one colour, often the slatey blue-green that is a favourite background colour in peasant homes. Grey was often used too, partly because it became so fashionable in the late eighteenth century, and partly because the ingredients – carbon black, chalk, with perhaps a touch of iron oxide red – were so widely available and therefore relatively inexpensive. Highly decorated pieces stood out particularly well against such muted backgrounds.

This detail from the interior opposite shows how many vivid colours have gone into creating the spattered finish, white, red-brown and vivid blue onto a pinky-ochre base. We can also see the order of application, first white, then red and blue. The long streaky spatters are made by dipping birch twigs rapidly into watery distemper and flicking it towards the wall in an upward movement, rather like a backhand stroke. Here it looks as if the painter flicked on white spatters to create a rough sort of trellis which he then filled in reasonably evenly with the red and touches of blue.

OPPOSITE *A provincial solicitor or doctor might have owned a room decorated and furnished like this sometime around the mid-nineteenth century. The most recent thing in the room would have been the spattered wall decoration, in the splashy style which had become fashionable because of its resemblance to wallpaper and was carried out in colours that were purely decorative and pleasing rather than studiously imitative of granites. Spattering – stenkmålning in Swedish – is best done with distemper paints, because these are absorbent enough for the spatter colour to sink in at once rather than trickling down.*

A craze for marbling began at this time. Marbling effects, running riot over beds, walls and furniture, were a sign that a family could afford to hire a painter, because it was generally accepted that special competence was needed to carry off such bold work. 'Farmer marbling', as the more bizarre and naïve styles are called, rarely looks like anything in the mineral world, but it is a highly decorative invention in its own right. Splashed across a wall of panelled alcove beds, on doors and cupboards, it has an exhilarating exuberance of colour and dashingly diagonal movement far removed from the homeliness we associate with wooden cottages. Since marbling persisted as long as *stuga* decoration did – well into the nineteenth century – one must assume that it was considered to give exceptional value. Perhaps painters urged it upon their clients; once the basic technique has been mastered, no paint effect is applied more quickly, or gives more impact for the money.

If marbling suggested grander interiors, other methods of dressing up a simple coat of paint caught on because, finally, they proved easy enough for anyone to take a hand. Wallpaper became fashionable in the early nineteenth century, but as most was imported it was expensive. In addition, it was difficult in timber houses to paper over the cracks in the board walls. With typical Scandinavian resourcefulness, simple paint tricks were used to create something of the all-over effect of printed wallpaper. Two of the most effective of these techniques are *stenkmålning*, a spatter technique using birch twigs and distemper colours, and *schablonmålning* or stencilling, a decorative device that Scandinavians have always used with exceptional skill and imagination.

In many cottage interiors the wallspace was divided into separate fields by a dado-style ruled line. This gave the painter the opportunity to use two colourful effects on the same wall. A favourite combination was to spatter below the dado in one set of muted colours (usually in imitation of granite), and to stencil stripes or lattice patterns in another set of colours above. One might suppose dadoes, as a formal decorative device, to be not at all suitable for rustic log cabins, but in fact many old Norwegian cabins were treated to this fashionable effect. Carried out in ochre above, and a sober dark blue below, as in one contemporary print, the result is surprisingly handsome, but some other interpretations, in rose pink and pale blue, look rather incongruous in their rugged, rough-hewn context.

Scandinavian peasant art changed slowly and evolved in an idiosyncratic way. By the eighteenth century peasant life in the region was relatively secure, even prosperous, hence the increased opulence of colour and decoration. Good ideas were rarely discarded because they had become unfashionable in the outside world, nor were the painters – craftsmen and amateurs – remotely concerned with aesthetic scruples about mixing one style with another. The furniture makers and painters of Ångermanland, the *kurbits* painters of Dalarna, and the decorative painters in the Norwegian *rosmålning* tradition pursued a stubbornly eclectic course, picking up and incorporating decorative novelties from the mainstream of European art whenever they came across them.

ABOVE *Busy marbling in a variety of styles but one overall burnt sienna tone covers the whole interior of a first-floor room in a wooden cottage in Värmland, Sweden. The marbling and* trompe-l'oeil *effects, alternating with pilasters and the unusual* trompe-l'oeil *mirror are restricted to canvas hangings.*

ABOVE *In complete contrast, a detail of the highly sophisticated early eighteenth-century marbling at Steninge. There are said to be thirteen distinct types of painted marble combined in the Oval salon, of which six are visible in the section of wall niche and pedestal photographed here.*

ABOVE *This marbling from the handsome dining room at Sturehov is a good half century later than the example from Steninge. Although just as sophisticated technically, it is more subtle, reflecting the refinement of Francophile taste at this time.*

ABOVE *Eccentric as this example of 'farmer marbling' from northern Sweden may appear in relation to geology, it is an effective solution to the difficulties of marbling with water-based distempers and, in its odd way, a very decorative one.*

ABOVE *Most of the tigerish marbling and graining in Frederiksborg Castle in Copenhagen was restored in the 1930s, but the section shown here, in a tiny anteroom, appears to be original, probably of the late seventeenth century, its bold colouring preserved by absence of light. Heavy marbling was fashionable at this period.*

ABOVE *Decidedly rustic, this marbling belongs to the scribble-and-slash style which was another solution to marbling with coloured distempers. It is hardly inspired as* trompe-l'oeil, *but nevertheless makes an effective foil to the fine corner cupboard whose dark blue panels are finished in a similarly scribbly style using oil paints.*

ABOVE *Marbling in this cool, unobtrusive style and colouring was the preferred fashion throughout Europe from the eighteenth century onwards, and remains the most popular style in general use in Scandinavia today, for foyers, banks and public buildings.*

ABOVE *Streak and splodge rather than slash and scribble, this dramatic panel of marbling comes from the extraordinary entrance hall to the small baroque manor of von Ekstedska Gården in Värmland, Sweden.*

OPPOSITE *Austerity softened by vivid decoration and kindly textures is a Scandinavian formula charmingly exemplified by this little bedroom with its kurbits wall decorations whose colours are exactly paralleled in the woven wool bed cover and picked up yet again in the Baltic blue paint used on the chair and table. The kurbits are of high quality, packed with sprightly incident. Experts can tell by the border motifs which village the painter came from in Dalarna, the copper-mining province in central Sweden which gave rise to this distinctive manifestation of rural or peasant art. Note especially here the bizarre leaf shapes on the wall behind, probably a rudimentary attempt at graining, as surreal in its way as the 'egg' or 'pebble' style marbling at Hembygsgården, pages 242–3.*

The early nineteenth century probably saw the *stuga* at its most charming, its basic austerity softened by vivid colour on walls and furniture, its scrubbed pine table-top and floor bleached to the colour of silver sand, a newfangled cast-iron or ceramic stove warming the interior more efficiently than the open fire and more cleanly, so that colours sang out as they were intended to instead of gradually disappearing under a sticky coat of soot. There might have been a rag rug or two for the floor, an oil lamp or a pretty china ornament, often Staffordshire, to stand on the chest of drawers or bureau grained to suggest fashionable mahogany, which became a prized item of furniture at this time. But by the end of the century, economic changes and emigration had left a depopulated countryside and many peasant dwellings lay abandoned and empty. These today, if they have survived long years of neglect, are bought as weekend and holiday homes by the newly prosperous Scandinavians who live in small modern city flats, drive shiny new Volvos and have some of the highest living standards in Europe. Of the cottages that remained inhabited, often by generation after generation of the same family, most have inevitably been modernized, and the 'naïve' folk decoration either painted over or removed during the craze for stripped pine in the 1960s. Life goes on and homes are not museums. There are probably still many decorated peasant interiors awaiting rediscovery and intelligent conservation. Until 'plastic paint' flooded the Nordic countries in the 1950s, overpainting was rarely irreversible; later coats of distemper can be soaked and scrubbed off, and oil-based paints removed with hot-air guns. There have been extraordinary discoveries: richly decorated walls and ceilings have been found hidden under false ceilings and streched canvas *tapeter*, or simply buried under layers of old paint. A new generation of *stuga* owners is learning to feel proud of this unique Scandinavian cultural inheritance instead of rejecting it as evidence of backwardness. These householders are more likely to spend hours patiently trying to restore such buildings to their former state, not from nostalgia necessarily, but because they can and do appreciate that the humblest stencilled border or spattered dado adds atmosphere because it is authentic, and because it expresses the essentially unpretentious, straightforward and intensely homely character of Scandinavia's old peasant cottages.

ROSMÅLNING

Anyone who feels inspired to try their hand at imitating the rich, exuberant patterns and warm colours of old decorated peasant furniture should look into the basic techniques of *rosmålning*. This remains the best documented of the country painting traditions, and is indeed still practised by professionals in the remote Norwegian valleys where the style first evolved.

As with so many crafts, more science or technique is involved than would appear from the fine freedom with scrolls, flowers, dots and teardrops have been dashed together to create a characteristic design. The freedom comes from knowing and using the right technique; a scroll or a teardrop begun at the wrong end, easily done when copying a design, will take four or five strokes to complete a shape that correct technique produces in one, and all fluency will be lost. By learning the right movements one is pointed in the right direction from the start.

Rosmålning literally means 'rose painting'. Highly stylized roses, or flowers, figure in most *rosmålning*

designs, but the meaning of the term has stretched to include, these days, most styles of Norwegian country painting. However, to a trained eye, *rosmålning* work by any of the old practitioners is immediately recognizable as being by a particular hand in a certain region at a particular time.

The twining movement of rosmaling patterns harks back to Viking 'ribbon' carving, of which examples survive on twelfth-century stave churches. But the scroll motif, the basic component in all large-scale designs, clearly derives from the classical acanthus motif which the Greeks carved into Corinthian capitals. It was recycled during the Renaissance, and became the favourite motif of eighteenth-century Norweign artists, who responded to the strong movement and clear-cut shapes to which this scallopped, fleshy plant lends itself, and translated it into carving, paint, metalwork and inlay. The acanthus motif could have reached Norway via an imported piece of Dutch marquetry, or via the work of a foreign crafts-

LEFT *Recent* rosmålning *decoration, in modern free-style colours, gives importance to a simple chest of drawers. The whole surface has been distressed with an antiquing glaze applied over finished decoration to soften and blend together bright primary reds and yellows with the pale blue background colour.*

BELOW *A close-up showing the construction of stylized motifs used in building up a* rosmålning *flowerpiece, or border.*

Rosmålning *decoration adorns the front and inner lid of this fine early nineteenth-century chest from Åseral, Norway. The central figure of Christ stands between two panels of flowers which show the characteristic sinuous twinings.*

man employed, as was commonly the case, on church decoration. What is certain is that this virile, springy, dynamic motif was an immediate source of inspiration to Norwegian craftsmen. It begins to appear in carved woodwork in stave church interiors of the baroque (*c.* 1700) period. The carved patterns were painted in strong traditional colours. It is easy to see how country painters, struck by the handsome, colourful shapes of the carved acanthus, would wish to re-create them with the paint on a flat surface. The earliest work in *rosmålning* style dates back to the beginning of the eighteenth century, but the style continued to develop regionally until the beginning of the twentieth century, when it went into a period of eclipse along with many other rural crafts. However, the skills were not forgotten even if there was no longer a commercial demand for the painted work. Thus a recent revival of interest, in the USA especially, has been able to draw on the experience of living practitioners of a style which has been over two centuries in the making. To watch a skilled professional go through the proper motions of setting out a *rosmålning* design immediately makes clear the importance of brushes and technique.

Rosmålning starts with the correct brush. The Telemark school of rosmalers use flat brushes in various widths, in red sable, for all main outline strokes. Flat brushes produce strokes with a greater variety of possible 'endings', and typical Telemark work is marked by a leaping asymmetry and surface variety. Hallingdal rosmalers

favour round red sable brushes throughout. These are usually found easier to handle by beginners, but this initial boost is offset by the Hallingdal emphasis on symmetry; what the round brush does easily on one half of the design is a great deal more difficult to repeat on the other. *Rosmålning* painters test each brush separately before buying; a good brush is resilient and the hairs snap back cleanly at the end of the stroke, flat with a flat brush, to a fine point with a round one. Sable is expensive, as painters know, but hairs of this quality are needed to absorb enough paint to complete a brush stroke. Surfaces to be decorated can be prepared with any good mid-sheen commercial paint, hard dry. But traditionally, Norwegian furniture, well made of mature pine with straight grain and few knots, would have had no filler or undercoat but rather several coats of thin oil colour applied direct to the wood. This oil colour was made of boiled linseed oil, turpentine, and dry pigment, with a little chalk added to certain pigments to speed drying. It requires many thin coats, with sufficient drying time between, to build up a strong colour such as the deep brown-reds, dull greens and strong blues favoured in *rosmålning* backgrounds, but the reward for such patience is an exceptionally lively surface with the wood texture just showing through. Having arrived at the base colour they were after, many of the old painters wiped a very thin film of oil/turpentine over the dry paint before beginning the *rosmålning* motifs; this gives brushstrokes more 'slip'.

The way the brush is held is equally important. Beginners feel happier the closer brushwork aproximates to writing; they like to come really close to the work, and make small, careful strokes rather slowly. This gives the illusion of control, but makes for weak, stiff, irresolute strokes. The master *rosmålning* painter stands or sits back from the work, using a long-handled brush held at the end of the handle. The free hand lends support to the brush hand, propping elbow or wrist, but the brush hand moves in a relaxed but controlled way, from a loose wrist; with practice (today's rosmalers practise on melamine, which can be wiped clean easily) this gives brushstrokes their own momentum, the weight of the brush and the viscosity of the paint between them complete the stroke.

As with any new language, it takes time and practice to acquire fluency with the brush, but new subtleties emerge the more one looks into the technique. 'Flat brush' scrolls, tapered one end and broadening to a fat 'hook' at the other, are done with the flat brush on its side to begin with, for the taper; increasing pressure while swirling the brush onto its flat side produces a majestic swelling curve 'hooked' by a slight backstroke just before lifting the brush off. Perfect circles are achieved with the flat brush by rolling the brush round with the thumb; when the brush has been loaded with two paint colours, the result is a bullseye, in one. Hallingdal round-brush strokes are less graphic, but more graceful, with an abundance of round-petalled daisy-like flowers, and expressive commas and dots. The round brush scroll shape is completed in two movements, starting at the finely tapering end and tracing the inner curve first: then without lifting off the brush, it goes into reverse and paints in the outer curve with a steadily decreasing pressure, till only the point is resting on the surface. Teardrops are formed with one short stroke, lifting the brush off cleanly. Teardrops radiating from a blob make a daisy; teardrops in one colour radiating from a still-wet blob of another pulls out the centre colour to make instant two-tone petals. Plump and perfect dots are easily made with the round brush. Load a little too much paint on the brush, so that it looks as if it might drip, press the tip lightly onto the surface and a professionally effortless dot remains. Cruder dots can be made with fingertips.

Country painting of this sort might be described as brush-led; in skilled hands the brush, as it were, thinks and invents, but always within its own vocabulary of strokes. The masters added greater variety by such devices as taking up two or more colours on one brush for a

OPPOSITE *The vibrant warm colours on this chest painted in the* rosmålning *style blend naturally with the softwood base material. The scroll-like ornaments and stylized flowers focus the eye on the owners' initials painted on the two central cartouches.*

LEFT *An old wooden food box decorated in* rosmålning *shows the intense but soft colours favoured in traditional 'rose painting'. Here English red and yellow ochre feature on a base of Prussian blue. Outlining in white, as well as whiskers of black, dramatize the springing shapes and give a lively spontaneity to the motif. Subtle shading with a dark glaze has been used to emphasize the leaves and petals as well as to soften the strong background blue.*

clear, clean two-tone effect. They also, in Telemark especially, used transparent or thinned paint colours so that the base colour glows through, giving a softer, ethereal look to the design. Alternatively, they might use the same thin-coloured glaze brushed over a whole design (dry) to intensify, modify, or 'antique' the colour scheme. This glaze work is known as 'lasur', *lasur* being Norwegian for glaze. Glaze manipulated in various decorative ways, as in marbling, stippling, ragging, made a patterned surround for intense passages of *rosmålning*. One sees this combination on much peasant furniture, and it is invariably effective, the looser rhythms of the *lasur* work balancing the more formal decoration in panels.

The final flourish in *rosmålning* – one common to most rustic painting – is 'outlining'. Outlining does more than emphasize existing shapes; it is used by rustic painters to give a flyaway vivacity to designs which might otherwise appear stolid. Using an outlining brush (often a sword liner with a long tapering tail of bristle), they outline some main shapes in a dark colour, adding crosshatching to the heart of a flower motif, and shoals of teardrops and dots around the main shapes. Then, using a light contrasting colour, the process may be repeated, but differently, with the addition of delicate 'whiskers' in the spaces,

stamens to flowers, or more dots or 'pearls' round the perimeter.

Anyone who has watched a professional at the 'outlining' stage finds the process spell-binding; a shower of flicks and dots and cross-hatching and what already looked a well-realized design takes wing. But it is also clear, comparing recent *rosmålning* with earlier work, that a seductive facility can be the undoing of rustic art. It is hard for an inspired brush to know when to leave off; outlining easily goes too far, too fast, and the robustness of the early tradition is lost under a shower of pretty grace notes. The built-in corrective, when rustic painting was undertaken seriously, and commercially, must have been profitability. Time was money, and over-elaboration led to smaller output and reduced profit. The tension set up by the need to produce impressive attractive, saleable work as fast as possible, was probably a healthy one, and resulted in the most assured, balanced use of designs and techniques. Thus, broad *lasur* effects (fast and impressive) counterpointing decoratively painted panels or centrepieces offer an ensemble in which the virtuoso technique of the craftsman and the brave colours enjoyed by a rustic clientele meet and marry with exhilarating effect.

PAINTED CHURCHES

When William Blake was in his teens he rounded a corner in Peckham Rye and saw a vision: a tree full of angels. Blake belonged to the company of mystics who find God everywhere, blazing out of ordinary insignificant things; all heaven, as he put it, in a grain of sand.

There is something Blakean, in their fusion of the ordinary and ecstatic, about the painted churches of Scandinavia. The contrast between the modest exterior of what is typically a small parish church of whitewashed stone, and the dazzle of painted decoration inside – wave upon wave of angelic hosts, bible stories and painted ornament ascending to the roof and covering, as often as not, every inch of the internal structure – is still breathtaking, as it was clearly intended to be when first painted anything up to nine hundred years ago. Some of these churches contain other treasures: statuary, splendid ironwork, crucifixes of extraordinary primitive pathos and carved granite fonts as massively simple as a giant's drinking cup. But the wonder these buildings inspire, and which catches at one's throat, is in their polychromy; this is Byzantium in paint, a poor man's Byzantium and all the more moving because of that.

The most ancient, and primitive, of the painted churches are the thirty or so Norwegian stave churches, built entirely of wood, which are all that remain of an estimated seven hundred and fifty that were put up in the eleventh century. (Christianity arrived in Scandinavia around the year 1000 brought back initially by Vikings or Norsemen from western European countries, including England.) The stave church at Heddal, which dates from the twelfth and thirteenth centuries, is almost a painted version of Blake's tree full of angels – its massive pillars of smooth pine support a wooden shell painted in glowing blue green, thick with painted figures and packed with swirling acanthus leaves.

Painted decoration of such loving elaboration is rare in the smaller parish churches of northern Europe, and its heartfeltness still communicates across the centuries, even to this secular and materialistic age. This magnificent decoration, by the famous Swedish artist, Albertus Pictor, is from Härkeberga church, *one of his masterpieces, painted in the fifteenth century, and shows his style at its most purely decorative, an ecstatic yet controlled crescendo of ornament as sumptuous, in its different way, as the beautifully organized colour and pattern of a Persian carpet.*

There is evidence that the earliest church buildings throughout Sweden were built, like the Norwegian stave churches, entirely or partly of wood, but that as more money became available – sometimes through the patronage of a local lord – they were often rebuilt in stone. Dadsjo church in Småland is one of the few to have kept its original wooden ceiling, painted in the late thirteenth century in glowing, jewel-like colours.

The earliest churches in Denmark were built of wood; at the beginning of the twelfth century, a number were built out of stone or granite. Although there were few quarries in Denmark, a good supply of surface boulders (in addition to quarries) were found in the Scanian provinces and the island of Bornholm, where there are some fine round stone churches. In other areas ice-age boulders were dug out from the clayey soil to provide building material.

The Nordic countries accepted Christianity quite readily and bloodlessly, although they kept on many of their pagan beliefs. To peasants leading brutally hard lives, the Christian message of equality and ultimate redemption finally held more comfort than the Viking cult of glory through valour; although missionaries had trouble overcoming a deep revulsion among their converts to the crucifixion, with its message of passive suffering. Judged by Viking standards Christ was a weakling, a God who let himself be put to death without a fight.

Heddal stave church is one of the most ancient wooden churches in Norway, surviving from the first wave of Christian proselytizing which began in the eleventh century in Scandinavia. Stave churches like Heddal, with their stiff shingle plumage and rakish carved finials strike an exotic note in their calm green valleys, but this style of construction is found wherever the 'conifer culture' stretched, from central Russia through central Europe as far as the west coast of Norway beyond the Baltic Sea. There is also a Viking influence about the carved decoration reminiscent of the raking prows of the streamlined wooden longships which put out to sea from Norway's fjords in earlier centuries.

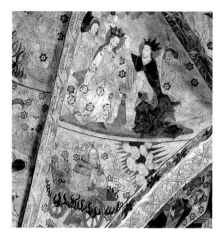

ABOVE *The delicacy of Albertus Pictor's colouring, and his prolific use of stencilled ornament in the shape of snowflakes and twining plant forms, is clearly shown in this detail from a painted vault at Härkeberga. The powdered stencils, one over the background, another decorating the Virgin's robe, were probably gilded originally with gold leaf that has tarnished or worn off.*

The evident purpose of painted decoration in churches was to amaze, instruct and enchant an illiterate congregation and convince them that the Christian God was all-powerful, and that the building they attended was, in literal truth, His House. The Uppland Law, an ancient Scandinavian text, insists on the sacredness of the building itself. 'No man shall worship false gods and no man put faith in groves and stones ... All shall honour the church: thither all shall go, the quick and the dead, entering the world and leaving the world.' Pagan Viking rites referred to in the same text survived well into the Christian period and, in a number of early Christian churches, Norse symbols, such as the ring representing sun worship, or dragon carvings, were incorporated into the Christian decorative scheme.

As an incentive to church building in the early expansionist period of Christianity, men were told that they could be accompanied to heaven by as many people as their churches would hold. Perhaps it is not surprising that early church paintings in Scandinavia tend to reinforce the dramatic contrasts of the Last Judgement, with the chosen ascending to celestial rewards accompanied by angels, while the damned, with hideously contorted faces, are dragged down to hellish torments.

There are scores of painted churches left in Scandinavia and they form an incomparable legacy, whether for scholars researching medieval iconography, or for those interested in getting closer to the

RIGHT *Polychromy fills every available space, using a considerable variety of decorative elements, in the interior of Härkeberga. The marbled organ loft would have been a late addition, painted in the same clear cerulean blue which Albertus chose as the dominant colour in his scheme for the church.*

The wall paintings at Tierps church are more faded and worn than at Härkeberga, but they are recognizably in the Albertus Pictor style, combining panels of figure painting with bracken-like fronds and bands of bold ornament which act as a frame visually as well as emphasizing architectural elements such as roof ribs and pillars. The marbled and gilt pulpit has the air of a later, seventeenth-century interpolation.

medieval spirit. The stave churches are perhaps the most exotic and astonishing buildings of all, their stiff plumage of wooden shingles giving them, in their green valleys, the appearance of tethered birds of prey at roost. The painted work in their interiors is on the whole less sophisticated but more vigorous than in the more notable Swedish churches such as Rada and Härkeberga. Other striking painted churches in Sweden include Sodra Rada, in Värmland, Taby in Uppland, Härkeberga and Tierps near Stockholm, Bjeresjo and Loederup near Lund, Edshult and Grenna in Småland, Rising near Linköping, Tegelsmora near Uppsala, and the churches at Floda and Solna. In Denmark the round churches of Nylars and Oster-Lars, on Bornholm, contain early polychrome painting and later work can be seen at Vallanbaek, Soborg and Ballerup, and in the side chapels of Roskilde cathedral.

Few of the early church painters are known by name; but, to judge from the traces of European influence seen in the work of this period, it seems reasonable to suppose that skilled painters from abroad followed in the train of proselytizing missionaries and recruited helpers on the spot, to whom they gradually passed on their skills. It is apparent that by the late fifteenth century, when church painting was dominated by Albertus Pictor (1440–1509) of Stockholm, native painters were well grounded in various decorative techniques.

A detail from Tierps showing its baroque woodwork and late medieval wall painting in quiet harmony. The handsome gilt frame to the right, with its own candle holder, contains a slab of slate with rows of hooks on which brass cut-out letters and numerals were hung, giving the chapter and verse for the Sunday lessons in question.

83

ABOVE *Repeat stencilling on the left and later marbling combined with gold leaf in this detail of the carved and painted altarpiece shown right. The curious brown 'shadow', which mimics the marbled outline with its painted scrolls, is a* trompe-l'oeil *device to add drama and chiaroscuro in a typically mannerist style, which also turns up in secular painted decoration of the period.*

RIGHT *Scandinavian medieval churches were almost bare of furnishings, and the congregation stood or knelt on the stone floor. The riotously and gorgeously decorated gallery pulpit and altarpiece shown in this photograph of Härkeberga would have been added later. The colourfulness of the painted finishes illustrated may have been a deliberate response to the earlier polychromy which can be seen beyond the pulpit. It is easy to see how rural painters and furniture makers would have been inspired by effects and colour-schemes as exuberant as these.*

Blueness, compounded of wintry northern light as well as a copious use of the pigment in marbling and wall painting, settles like a mist over this long view of Härkeberga taken from beneath the organ loft with its attractive pendentive trim. An early carved figure of the crucified Christ makes a poignant and dramatic centrepiece at the threshold to the altar. Painted marbling is almost invariably the finish chosen to decorate church furniture, such as the pews shown here, all over Scandinavia. It was obviously seen as adding dignity and usefully broken colour which would conflict less with existing polychrome decoration.

ABOVE *The pale but vivid cerulean blue which contrasts so interestingly with ochre and purple brown, closely resembles a limewash shade which in England was known as 'bice'. It is possible that medieval church painters in Scandinavia used a combination of limewash colours, applied in the 'fresco secco' technique, over large areas filling in detail with distemper colours.*

Records show that Albertus completed the internal decoration for one medium-sized church every season, which would have been impossible had he not had a team of assistants working under him. His most famous work is found in the churches at Harkeberga and Kumla and here the complex polychrome decoration covers walls, vaults and the roof ribs. Although some of the decoration has perished, the overall effect is intense but controlled and still radiantly luminous. The use of colour is very subtle and the colour harmonies are surprisingly delicate. The draughtsmanship is fine, combining a distinctive style with a great range of feeling. For the modern observer, however, the chief interest of Albertus' wall paintings lies in the vivid characterization of the figures – some of them dressed in the height of fifteenth-century fashion, with long, pointed boots, belted jerkins and rakish felt hats pulled down over flowing locks. A sense of reverence and spirituality is expressed in a tender representation of the Virgin, seated on a golden crescent with an aureole of golden rays, giving suck to the infant Jesus perched naked on her beautifully draped lap. The Last Judgement is sombre and moving; Christ gravely displays his pierced hands and feet to his kneeling disciples while angels trumpet and tiny naked figures rise from their graves, hands clasped beseechingly, awaiting judgement. Elsewhere, the moral of the scene is a little obscured by the liveliness of the composition, with vividly characterized individual figures riding the wheel of life, feasting and drinking, shouldering a longbow, or, in the case of a jester in cap and bells, fingering a lute. This is a world that seems to look forward to Brueghel, and it is tempting to think that it must have been intended to entertain the congregations as much as to edify them.

RIGHT *Something of the animation of murals of Albertus Pictor can be sensed from this ceiling detail, where lively figures in medieval garb of parti-coloured tights and felt caps are interspersed with more conventional figures – crowned virgins and the haloed saints and disciples of Christian iconography.*

87

Stronger and simpler contrasts, favouring darker colours, are a characteristic feature of seventeenth-century baroque church painting. As walls became plainer, often simply whitewashed, ceilings and furnishings became correspondingly ornate, often compartmented, as here, and filled in with 'Continental style' painting which tends to hover between secular and religious in its intention. The pair of cherubs here look more like pagan cupids than winged seraphs.

It is not known how Albertus received his training. He may well have been apprenticed to a church painter, possibly a German. German influence can be seen in the iconography of some of his scenes; these were based on the woodcut illustrations to the *Biblia Pauperum*, which was illustrated and printed in Germany. The delicacy of Albertus' line recalls the best German drawing of his day, but his ebullient use of colour and ornament, and flashes of humorous observation, are characteristically Nordic.

As was common practice, Albertus Pictor made use of standard patterning tools such as templates and stencils that enabled the purely repetitive work to be carried out by assistants. Details such as stencilled gilt stars were powdered – spaced out on a regular grid – over the background to figures, and ornamental borders, used to frame biblical scenes, were stencilled in two or more colours. Templates were also used to block-in some of the large-scale figures in Albertus' decorative schemes. Such templates were in widespread use and in many wall paintings all ten Wise and Foolish Virgins, or the procession of Magi on horseback, share the same outline.

In 1523, not quite twenty years after Pictor's death, Gustavus I Vasa launched the Reformation in Sweden, financed with a loan from the Hanse merchants. Ten years later Christian III of Denmark followed suit, and the two monarchs were able to confiscate church lands and property and set themselves up as heads of the new Lutheran state religion.

Churches did not change overnight, although the forms of worship did. In general, the transition occurred smoothly, without arousing fanatical protest on either side, although the peasantry seem to have surreptitiously kept up the Catholic observances that mattered to them, adding for instance a stylized Ave Maria monogram to their festive ornaments for centuries after the Reformation. Some church interiors were painted over, to bring them into line with the new Lutheran aesthetic, but a surprising number of interiors survived intact. More whitewashing was done in Denmark than elsewhere, but the Norwegian stave church of Oye was taken apart, piece by piece, and hidden beneath the floor of the Lutheran church that replaced it.

Luther's tolerance of painted images, as long as they were of religious subjects and conveyed a proper reverence for the Creation, meant that painting was not banished from newly built or re-modelled protestant churches. Polychrome decoration was used in Norwegian seventeenth-century churches, but in Sweden and Denmark churches began to present a plainer appearance, with whitewashed walls and clear glass windows. In the decorative schemes carried out in Swedish churches of that time, colour was mainly confined to the ceilings, which were elaborately painted in the style first seen around the middle of the seventeenth century at Läckö Castle, with grisaille work imitating sculpted plaster wreaths surrounding compartments and roundels containing painted scenes. In churches these contained biblical scenes treated in the newly fashionable style with dramatic lighting effects, masses of swirling clouds and figures modelled in light and shade. Rich colours, made possible by the use of oil-based paint, replaced the delicate chalky washes of fresco and distemper.

The ambitiousness of such attempts to paint in the heroic style of the European masters of the day put considerable strain on the skill of many Scandinavian church painters. The earlier tradition, with its stylization and absence of modelling, gained a touching simplicity from the *naïveté* of some of its practitioners. The new style, with its demands for greater realism, made the weaknesses of some provincial painters appear comic. Painters had difficulties with hands, feet and facial expressions. A favourite device for disguising weak spots was the use, wherever possible, of turbulent, rolling clouds, resembling nothing so much as cauliflowers. At Mossebo church the Ascension is depicted by the underside of Christ's feet being swallowed by a cloud bedecked with winged cherub heads. However, if one does not look at the decoration too closely, and it is after all up on the ceiling (often painted directly on to the boards), the general effect is colourful and exuberant, and contrasts well with the impressive grisaille panels that surround it, the plain whitewashed walls and the marbled finishes.

Marble finishes for pillars, pews, altar rails and pulpit became fashionable around this time. The leading architect Nicodemus Tessin the Elder launched marbling as an *illusionmålning* finish in his work for the Royal Palaces, and it rapidly became a leading element in all decorative schemes – religious as well as secular – of the period. Tessin's early marbling was in a discreet palette of black and white on pale grey, but by 1700 his son Tessin the Younger had devised a patriotic marbling finish in subdued green tones taken from Sweden's only natural marble, Kolmard. Cool-toned marbling was quite often combined with dark graining, in imitation of precious hardwoods such as mahogany and walnut.

Later whitewash may have blanked out medieval decoration here, but this is as likely to have been done to cover over dilapidation as in a mood of puritan revolt against decoration and colour. The Reformation was established more peacefully in the Scandinavian countries than elsewhere in Europe, notably Britain.

89

Farms and Manors

The relative outward uniformity of wooden housing lends some colour, at least in rural areas, to the notion of Scandinavian countries as one-class societies, and makes it easy for foreign visitors to miss the finer social distinctions. For instance there is a difference in Sweden between the *bondagård*, or farmer farm, and the *herrgård*, or gentleman farm. These correspond to a working farm and a small manor house standing in its own estate. Externally, both categories of farm may look considerably alike: long, low, wooden buildings with a vaguely classical porch placed symmetrically in the middle of the front elevation. The whole building is probably painted Falun red, with crisp white detailing on the porch and window-frames. Size may or may not be a clue to status: on the whole an upper storey is an indication of superior social standing, yet von Ekstedska Gården, in western Sweden, built in the late seventeenth century by a *nouveau riche* royal functionary thought to have amassed a fortune by peculation, is in effect an extended bungalow. Conversely, more plebeian farmhouses have often donned an upper storey, along with other marks of gentility like carved porches and slate roofs, in a sudden rush of prosperity. The likelihood is that in most periods the lesser gentry of Scandinavia was, as in other European countries, in a state of flux. Upward mobility depended on individual energy and acumen, good harvests, or good fortune.

It is hard to imagine a more romantically Scandinavian interior than this extraordinarily satisfying mélange of fine darkened seventeenth-century painted decoration contrasted with the cool linden green of the draped bed and the matt washed leather texture of bare scrubbed floorboards. While the wall paintings are on canvas tapeter, or hangings, ceiling decorations in the grisaille manner are painted directly on to boards, a Scandinavian practice which sounds outlandish but in practice adds considerable charm. This room is from Skogaholm, a small manor now at Skansen, in Stockholm.

Open fireplaces, often set in courses like this small hearth at Kristoff's farm, near Gävle, were the only form of heating until the advent of the huge ceramic stoves, or 'kakelungen', which must have transformed people's existence during the long Scandinavian winters. Usually these simple plastered hearths are plainly whitewashed, obviously a regular attention to cover soot and stains, but occasionally they were carefully painted in imitation of Delft or other decorated tiles.

From a distance the main house may be obscured by the encircling farm buildings, which present an anonymous and often windowless expanse of tarred wooden sheds. The approach into the inner yard, which is frequently cobbled with immense granite setts, may be through a gap in the outbuildings, or, more impressively, through an archway which punches through stabling and barns. Once within, the *bondagård* declares itself unmistakably as the tallest of the many buildings facing the yard, at the far end of the sweep of cobbles across which duck-boards may be laid in bad weather. The farmhouse is often flanked on either side by smaller dwelling-houses, usually one storey high, but provided with details, such as porches and symmetrical windows, to distinguish them from the farm buildings. These smaller dwellings may include a house for old people, where ageing parents retire leaving the management of the farm to a son and his family, or a sister or brother's house, for siblings involved in running the farm, or, and this is a peculiarly Scandinavian phenomenon, a special building or *gillestuga* set aside for parties, feasts and family events, such as weddings, funerals and confirmations, and for entertaining visitors and guests during the summer months. This deliberate separation of hospitality from everyday family and domestic life can puzzle foreign visitors, who may misread it as ceremonious and stiff, similar to the old British working-class style of living as a family in the warm kitchen but receiving visitors in an icy, sombre, unused front room. In fact it goes back to the time when rural life was isolated and all visitors were welcome as they brought with them a breath of the outside world. Special guests, who might have travelled long distances, were properly honoured by a household showing its best face, with the finest linen on the beds, the best china and glass on display, a wealth of candles, festive costumes and, naturally, a rural banquet, at which, after liberal ritual doses of ale, schnapps or *brannvin* everyone present must have been very merry. This deep concern for outward form and for doing things properly, in the accepted fashion, is still a Scandinavian characteristic: a casual dinner in a centrally-heated, modern flat will be accompanied by candles standing in floral wreaths, the best china and glass and an anxious attention to detail.

Exotic palm trees and sunny blue skies framed by brightly draped columns turn out on closer inspection to be a northern Swedish painters' vision of Calvary and the crucifixion. From the party room or stor stuga at Kristoff's farm, this beguilingly primitive painted decor represents Swedish peasant taste at a modest level from the early nineteenth century. Characteristic details include the simple muslin pelmets, stripe runners and swivel-backed bench.

The last rays of sunset gild the window panes of this old wooden house at Bollstabruk so warmly that one might imagine the rooms were candlelit. Lighted windows are especially magical in winter snow and darkness. Even today it is customary to stand a small lamp in the front window of a Scandinavian cottage to throw a welcoming beam, and on feast days, such as Saint Lucia's Day or Christmas Day, porches and windowsills twinkle with constellations of lighted candles.

The ubiquitous Falun red seen at its ruddiest against fresh spring grass in this view of a typical barn and outbuilding on a Swedish farm. Thatched roofs usually have the pegged silhouette shown here, a defence against wind and snow. In other regions turf might substitute for thatch.

At closer quarters, one sees that the working farm and the gentleman's farm are mainly differentiated externally by the arrangement of their buildings and the way in which these are grouped in the landscape. The working farm, or *bondagård* – *bonda* in Swedish meaning a free, independent yeoman with the ancient right to a voice in national affairs via elected representatives of the Fourth Estate – is an extension of the typical peasant *stuga*, or cottage, but it has usually developed in a functional way, with all the subsidiary buildings grouped round a central courtyard, over which it presides, conspicuous in both size and detailing.

The *herrgård*, or gentleman's farm (*Friherr* is a form of address meaning baron) usually has a more formal aspect than the *bondagård*, to indicate the dwelling place of real gentry. It may stand on a rise in the ground and be reached by a short avenue of lime, birch or, in Denmark, beech. In Sweden, which has no fewer than 96,000 lakes, there is a good chance that one outlook of the *herrgård* will be over water. There is a practical as well as an aesthetic reason for this preference for siting houses near water: roads were often a less reliable form of transport than water, which could be crossed by boat in summer and by sledge when it was frozen over in winter. Beatelund, a rather grand *herrgård* on one of the cluster of islands near Stockholm called the Archipelago, has its own jetty, marked by two flagpoles, where visitors land who have taken the boat ride from Stockholm.

OPPOSITE *A corner of the entrance hall to the early eighteenth-century manor of Beatelund shows the exquisite effect that can be achieved with painted wall-hangings (tapeter) in the 'verdure' style combined with subtle toned paintwork and a floor of local purple-brown slate. The hangings shown here, original to Beatelund, were sold at auction along with the house and its contents early this century. Happily the buyer of the* tapeter *was shrewd, or imaginative, enough to offer them back to Beatelund's new owners who re-installed them with admirable taste, adding furniture and paintings in keeping with the mood of this highly picturesque setting.*

ABOVE *A detail gives a good idea of the technique used to paint wall-hangings in the* tapeter *manner, using distemper colours on canvas or linen, as here. Very often at a later date these* tapeter *were simply turned back to front, and newly decorated to keep up with changing fashions. Earlier and more picturesque subjects have sometimes come to light during modern repairs or alterations, turned to face the wall and thus inadvertently kept in an ideal state of preservation for a couple of hundred years.*

OPPOSITE *Faded Aubusson-type colours suggest that this eighteenth-century painted wall hanging from Skogaholm may have been imitating a later style of tapestry than the verdure type at Beatelund. However, decorated painted 'panels' are also the fashionable wall treatment in the latter part of the century, so this pretty and refined scheme is a happy blend of both ideas. The freshness of striped ticking upholstery adds a typically understated charm to the long sofa. Note how the wooden floor is set into a surround of green slate.*

BELOW *This detail from the interior opposite is rococo painted decoration of great elegance. Two or three 'panels' in this style are all that is needed to give distinction and finish to the simplest room. Scandinavian painters were excellent at inventing new and pretty variations on this theme. This is a decoration idea which deserves to be reinstated to lend character to uninteresting modern rooms, or restore suitable atmosphere to period rooms.*

The main difference between the interiors of the two types of rural home we are looking at reflect a difference in social standing between the owners. The *Friherr* faced out towards a wider world of society and international politics, connected to it – in the way of country gentry elsewhere – through a network of family relationships. The yeoman farmer's concerns, perhaps, were more locally bounded. As he grew prosperous he might have added extra rooms, or extra buildings, but furnished them in a thriftily functional manner, with decorative sorties confined to ornamented rustic furniture and painted hangings, which were brought out of storage and pinned up round the feast table for family celebrations and religious and other festivals. The most celebrated of these hangings, of which a remarkable number survive, are the curious *kurbits* paintings produced by provincial artists in the central Swedish province of Dalarna over two centuries or more. Painted at first on canvas or linen, later on cardboard, these usually portray Biblical stories in a vivid and crowded narrative style that seems to anticipate comic strips. *Kurbits* is thought to be a garbled version of the German word *kurbiss* – met with in the Lutheran Bible of the time – which means exotic plant or vine. (The prophet Jonah sat under one to shelter from the desert sun). One can guess how the thought of blazing sunshine and miraculous growth would operate on the imagination of an artist working in northern latitudes: the result is the great fertility symbol of the *kurbits*, an explosively arching cornucopia of flowers, which fills the sky over the heads of the Wise and Foolish Virgins, or looms above the smartly dressed young couple setting out hand in hand under the equivocal inscription 'We are going to enjoy ourselves for a while'. Fruits of the womb and fruits of the earth are equally desirable and inseparable in the peasant philosophy, and the *kurbits* symbol is introduced into these vignettes of peasant life masquerading as pious tales, with a sly humour, like an unrepentant double entendre from a pagan past. Certainly this must be how the Swedish poet Erik Karlfeldt interprets them, in one of a series of poems about the 'kurbits hangings':

> See my kurbits
> Its rise and shape
> Higher and higher it goes
> A most gorgeous thing
> From the land where the sun lives.

To left and right of the vivid little pull-out bed (its style a quaint blend of Gustavian neo-classicism with the religiose effect of a row of tiny black crosses) hang kurbits *paintings from the first part of the nineteenth century, painted by itinerant painters from Dalarna wandering westwards in search of summer commissions.*

The droll figures, in contemporary dress, and curious buildings (not unlike the traditional lusthus *or garden pavilion) are quite standard* dramatis personae *in this little-known school of naif painting, along with the floating bouquets, like rocketing flower arrangements.*

This celebrated interior, the hallway
to the small wooden baroque manor
house of von Ekstedska Gården, in
north-west Sweden, epitomizes a sort
of innocent gusto in its style of
decoration which is perhaps unique
to its place and time, and without
parallel in the more knowing
decorative tradition of Continental
Europe. There was evidently a vogue
for painted figures standing sentinel

in earlier eighteenth-century houses,
as the huntsmen and Cavaliers at
Sandemar, but the uniformed
grenadiers standing guard either side
of this rustic hallway are subtly
absurd (their feet cut off by the
skirting) in a way which suggests
they were added more for
amusement, a talking point, than
any other reason.

While the farmer kept such treasured ornaments as painted wall-hangings put away in chests or cupboards between family occasions, together with the trousseau of woven or embroidered cloths which made an answering splash of colour along shelves, beams and dresser fronts, the gentleman and his family were commissioning colourful decoration of a more permanent sort. The style is one of virile contrasts: crude but powerful patterns and strong but seasoned colour schemes. There is much use of *marmorering* or marbling, on woodwork, doors and dadoes, in colours that would make a geologist blink. Deep blue (blue being the expensive and therefore the most prestigious pigment of the day) on greyish white is a favourite. But in one *herrgård* in Norway there is a magnificent marbling treatment of a door and architrave in iron-oxide red on white, with dark blue used to pick out the mouldings, the heavy iron hinges and the latch. The marbling style follows the usual strong diagonal treatment, with meandering red stripes and curious red leaf shapes breaking up the white background. The effect is unlike anything found in nature, but it is both vigorous and handsome and must have given its first owners repeated pleasure every time they walked through it. To balance these strong effects on walls, floors were frequently painted to imitate chequered marble flags. These are usually executed in black and white and painted over the existing wide floorboards – cracks and all – with no attempt to disguise the subterfuge. Such floor treatments were reserved for rooms with formal aspirations: ballrooms in the grander houses, libraries in palaces, the salon or drawing room in the homes of the gentry.

Provincial taste is full of surprises, as this corner of a room at the Norwegian manor Fosseholm, near Oslo, altogether confirms. The whole striking but curiously uninhabited air of this room, with its eccentric decoration, is surely closer to one of Magritte's intense and surreal interiors than the Norwegian upper middle-class milieu which it apparently represents. One would have said it was a stage set rather than a real place, partly because of the blankness of the yellow wall and the uncomfortably vivid magenta sofa, partly because the marbled door is surely awaiting the entrance of a player left of stage.

OPPOSITE *A whole mysterious and foreign elegance is encapsulated in this austere but sensuous interior at Skansen, in Stockholm. Sparsely but nobly furnished, these astonishing living spaces are at once minimal and romantic, sculptural in the way they respond to the oblique Scandinavian light. One of the mysteries of eighteenth-century interiors of this style is the way they can be so empty, stripped to essentials, without appearing bleak and incomplete. The fine bureau and stove both help to people their space, but the subtle painted rococo wall decoration also adds its quota of atmosphere. All in all an object lesson to anyone who imagines that period rooms must be stuffed with artefacts.*

The *herrgård*, then, stands a little aloof from the farm itself, in its own garden with a separate approach; the farm buildings are hidden away beyond the trees. It aspires to dignity, and there are customary embellishments like gateposts, clipped yews and carved pilasters each side of a massive front door studded with iron nails. Older and more rustic *herrgårdor* may be painted with Falun red, but those built towards the end of the eighteenth century in the neo-classical style introduced by Gustav III may have shallow carved pilasters, painted white, applied at regular intervals to boarded walls painted creamy yellow. The occasional wooden manor house achieves a modest elegance reminiscent of early frame houses in East Coast towns in the United States; more often they have the slightly gauche charm of a house embroidered on a sampler.

The interiors of both farms and manors inevitably share many features, being built in much the same way using the same materials, and having a common descent from the peasant *stuga*. Both have superb floors of scrubbed pine boards throughout, and polite visitors remove their outdoor shoes on entering the building as in Japanese homes. The resemblance between farms and manors is stronger in older buildings, which are characterized by small rooms with low ceilings, often boarded, with paintwork in strong, deep colours. Visually these find their equivalent in the snug, wainscotted, soberly painted rooms with shuttered windows that create an atmosphere of solid bourgeois comfort in merchants' houses throughout Europe in the late seventeenth and early eighteenth centuries – and it is a fact that German and Dutch bourgeois styles entered Scandinavia via Denmark and the Baltic ports during this period.

RIGHT *Both regional and Anglophile, judging from the style of furniture and prevalent woodiness, this is the sort of late eighteenth-century interior associated with cities, and the homes of wealthy merchants, rather than the country homes of aristocratic families, where a certain cult of rusticity was considered appropriate. Interiors of this kind, snug and polished, in the manner of gentlemanly cabinets and offices in European cities, are in a minority in Scandinavia.*

MARBLING

The Romans imitated marble in paint, and it is likely that the use of this most prestigious of faux finishes reaches back further still, through classical Greece to ancient Egypt. What is certain is that it has been almost uninterruptedly the most popular of all the illusionist paint finishes during those historical periods – the Renaissance, the seventeenth century, the latter part of the nineteenth century – when such effects were admired, approved, and extensively used. There are many good reasons for this, both aesthetic and sociological. Marble – a crystalline limestone capable of taking a high polish – is powerfully decorative in itself, occurring in almost every conceivable colour combination, and an apparently inexhaustible variety of patterning: spotted, streaked, striped, veined, blotched, clouded. Nature has created a marble, it would seem, for every situation and all tastes, from fierce to dainty, bizarre to bland.

The sheer handsomeness of marble inevitably stimulated imitation, especially once painters discovered how readily these freakish inventions of nature lent themselves to imitation via paint. In practised hands, and this is a point not sufficiently understood by the layman perhaps, marbling is a comparatively rapid way of variegating and breaking up large areas of paintwork. An impressionistic sketch of the real thing, confidently dashed in with a feather or flexible brush, is all that is needed to give a noble and convincing effect. In some respects the imitation is even an improvement on the original. Setting aside questions of relative cost, painted marble has a softness which makes it a friendly surface to live with. Too much real marble can be hard, chilly and tomb-like, as well as deafeningly reverberant. Decoratively speaking a painted marble can be adapted to its context, reduced to an abstract doodle, softened to a gentle blur, or worked up to a theatrical intensity.

In countries such as Italy and France, with their abundant deposits of coloured marbles, the painted marbles were always to a certain extent competing with, and devalued by, the presence of the genuine article. In Scandinavia, however, indigenous marbles are a rarity, and the range of their colouration limited. Marbling in paint did not really get into its stride in Scandinavia till the seventeenth century, but it immediately achieved star status among the painterly techniques and has remained desirable, a status symbol as well as a decorative convention,

to this day. Travelling around Scandinavia one finds marbling everywhere, in private houses and public buildings, cottages and palaces, on doors and benches, pillars and rush-seated chairs. Much of the later work is of the highest technical quality, indistinguishable from real siena, verd antique, rouge roi and other genuine marble. This exact imitation is in the painstaking mode of nineteenth-century 'scientific' marblers, newly tuned into geological formations in the wake of such writers as John Ruskin. But it is the other tradition of Scandinavian marbling, of varying competence but unflagging invention, rustic verging on primitive in style, that catches the unprepared visitor by surprise. Scandinavian marbling of this sort can be found at all social levels, and is much too individual to be classified readily, but tends to be bold, stylized and non-naturalistic, for the good reason that it was often painted by someone who had never seen real marble, though they might have heard it described. Some of the wilder improvisations on the marbling theme, resembling unravelled knitting or strings of sausages, are most easily explicable as imagination working on hearsay. Once marbling became a feature of Scandinavian church decoration, during the seventeenth century, an accessible model was provided for the sort of decorative painters who learned by doing, possibly recruited to help with large decorative projects in their neighbourhood under the direction of a more skilled professional. However, lacking immediately available visual references and working from memory, many painters evolved fantastic marbling styles of their own, creating out of their ignorance, or innocence, a fascinatingly diverse family of painted effects whose resemblance to crystalline limestone may be tenuous but whose decorative impact is undeniable. The generic name given to such naïve marbling in Sweden is 'farmer marbling', which indicates the social level at which such painterly tricks had their greatest success. Despite this, such tidy categories tend to overlap in these underpopulated northern countries, and farmer marbling turns up in grander buildings, such as manor houses and town halls, in the remoter provinces. In their impressionistic way these examples constitute a valuable counterpoint to the slavishly naturalistic school of 'imitationmalning'. Ironically, the bizarre charm of such freestyle decorative work is now most likely to appeal to a highly sophisticated milieu. Marbling is still a popular decorative finish in Scandinavia today, but the emphasis is on technical excellence, verisimilitude. The foyers of nineteenth-century buildings now converted into business premises are regularly marbled in this style. As yet Scandinavia has been slow to appreciate, or develop, the eccentric and yet wonderfully vivid and varied effects pioneered by their own school – if something so personal could be grouped into a school – of rustic decorative painters. There is a rich seam here of proven decorative effects begging to be re-examined.

A simple country chair, vividly marbled in blue and white in a style which became fashionable in Sweden in the eighteenth century, stars in the room set built up out of the various paint techniques demonstrated and photographed for this book. The original chair which provided the inspiration for this effect, is rush-seated, from the rococo period, and can be seen in Stockholm's Nordisk Museet.

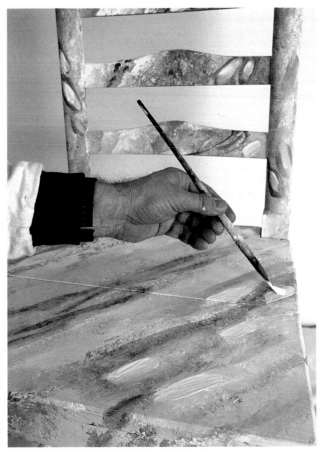

A sponge dipped in white oil-based undercoat is used to soften and break up the hardness of blue streaking and veining while it is still wet.

White 'pebble' shapes are added with a slender brush to further open up and variegate the blue surfaces.

The marbled chair which inspired the treatment shown here can be seen in Stockholm's Nordisk Museet, and the marbling is in the style known as Swedish rococo. This style, characterized by a monochromatic use of green, blue or grey-blue with lead white, and a sparing and light touch with the marbled effects, seems to derive from the specifically Swedish tradition of marbling based on the native Kolmard stone, which was developed by the Tessins for their decoration of Stockholm's Royal Palace. Variants on the style can be found all over Sweden, but especially in churches, where it is used to decorate pews, organ lofts, galleries and so forth. The original chair is ladder backed and straight legged, a modest provincial type of chair to which a rapid touch of grey-blue marbling

lends considerable charm. That it was rapid is an educated guess based on the fact that the copy shown here was completed in under twenty minutes, and is if anything more heavily marbled than the original.

Rococo marbling of this sort was more often done with linseed-oil paint, especially on furniture or on wood generally, because this resulted in a more durable finish as well as allowing veining and streaking to become more delicate. Compared with the bold zigzag effects dictated by the use of distemper paints for marbling, rococo marbling in oil has an airy, wispy quality in perfect harmony with 'rocaille' ornament.

The chair shown, which is almost identical to the Nordisk Museet original, was first undercoated in standard

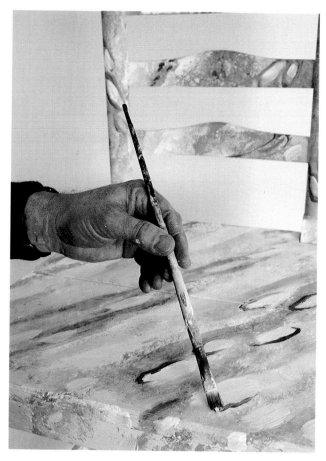

With the same brush and darker blue, pebbles are outlined and some of the veining emphasized.

The completed chair, minus a final coat or two of varnish. The entire process should not take more than half an hour.

white undercoat faintly dirtied with raw umber to match the colour of old lead white. Tones of Prussian blue mixed with the same undercoat were used for the marbling. The first step was to rapidly brush thinned white undercoat over the areas to be marbled. Into this wet white Prussian blue was applied, in a strong diagonal movement, using a brush and sponge for variety, and this was lightly softened with brush tips and a rag to break up the shapes a little. White pebbles were dotted in here and there with a fitch among the blue areas, and these were then outlined in darker blue with a sword liner, a small flexible rat-tail brush which is excellent for painting either straight or curved lines, because the thicker end picks up more paint than a fine sable brush, while the long rat tail

allows colour to be drawn out very finely and with control.

For a more delicate rococo finish, the chair or other surface might be painted first with two or three coats of traditional linseed-oil paint, using zinc white lightly greyed with black and raw umber. When dry the surfaces could be wiped over with an oil/turpentine glaze, and marbling brushed and sponged into the wet glaze, lightly and sparingly in the chosen colour, and then lightly softened by brushing across the lines and shapes with brush tips. This approach will give a fragility to the decoration which is typically rococo. The piece should be varnished with one or two coats of matt colourless varnish, thinned a little each time with turpentine or white spirit.

SPATTER PAINTING *(STENKMÅLNING)*

Of all the decorative painting techniques used so freely in Scandinavian interiors at every social level, none is more popular, or more peculiarly Scandinavian, than spatter painting or *stenkmålning* (Swedish, pronounced 'shtenk-mawlning'). One could hardly say they invented the technique, nor do they lay claim to it, but the Scandinavian painters have certainly extracted the last spot of decorative potential from the inherently simple idea of flicking spots of coloured paint over walls. One sees the technique in old cottages, new apartments, bank foyers, even the Haga Pavilion. It is sometimes combined with stencilling, more frequently with marbling. Usually it is done in quiet colours, say blue-black and white on pale grey, using an even spatter to just distress the wall surface without being obtrusive. But one also comes across wild combinations of colours spattered in skeins and loops looking rather like action painting. The appeal of spatter painting is that anyone can do it, but that the utterly simple means can also be made to yield quite complex and subtle effects. Add to this that the process is cheap, quick and visually very effective, and it is clear why it has become a classic Scandinavian finish.

Inspiration for *stenkmålning* is not far to seek in the Nordic world, where every rock outcrop consists of granite boulders, speckled in tones of pink, grey and brown. Porphyry, which used to be quarried in the north of Sweden, offers a richer mix of spattered colour, less often met with because of its rarity and cost, but was a popular stone for mausoleums, plinths, pedestals and smaller objets d'art. However it seems likely, to judge from the dates of early examples, that it was first used to mimic wallpaper at a period when wallpaper was imported, expensive, and a status symbol. This was during the 1820s in Scandinavia generally, though elegant hand-blocked papers were being imported from France, England and Germany a century earlier, for decorating fashionable houses. Wallpaper became cheap enough for ordinary people with the invention of roller printing, and released a wave of popular longing for loudly patterned walls. But there were always people who either could not afford wallpaper, however cheap, or whose plank or log walls made it unsuitable. Thus, perhaps, the spread of decorative paint effects which gave a busy texture and some colour to any surface.

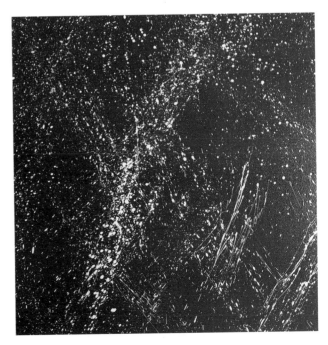

Stenkmålning is traditionally done with a small bundle of thin, whippy birch twigs bound together with twine, a fact which firmly stamps it as Scandinavian. One bundle of twigs was used for each colour in the spatter sequence. Birch twigs give a more distinct, well separated and irregular spatter of colour than the fine spray of dots produced by jogging a brush handle against a block of wood, the method commonly used by decorative painters elsewhere.

Walls were prepared for spattering with several coats of distemper, the cheapest and most easily made domestic paint. Distemper covers well and dries with a soft powdery bloom which is extremely attractive, though the high chalk content means that it rubs off easily. However, it produces clear and pretty pastel colours, and can be slapped on fast with one of the old fashioned round distemper brushes. Popular background colours for *stenkmålning* finishes were pearl grey, Stockholm white (which contemporary decorators call dirty white), pale blue, apple green, ochre yellow, and the subtle shade – grey in some lights, pink in others – Norwegians call *gammel rosa*, or old pink.

The spattering was done with the same distemper paint, tinted in two or three contrasting colours which usually included white. A pearl grey ground spattered with black and white is a favourite combination, giving a suggestion of grey granite; another, warmer effect was arrived at by spattering buff with white, brown-red and black. Each spatter colour modifies the base colour slightly, and the spatter colours interact with each other. Professional painters probably worked from sample boards, while the ordinary person imitated an effect seen somewhere else.

To make spatters the birch twigs are dipped into the colour – one colour goes on at a time – and then shaken slightly to clear loose drops, which would tend to splash. Then the birch whisk is shaken briskly towards the wall surface, leaving a constellation of coloured freckles. Standing closer to the wall produces a tighter spatter of smaller dots, while standing back tends to disperse the paint more widely and give a variegated spatter.

When all that was required was a softening and decorative effect, *stenkmålning* was done almost casually, leaving a great deal of the base colour showing, with no attempt to go for evenness. This type of finish suggests wallpaper. When there was a serious attempt to imitate stone, the spattering is much more intense and evenly spread over the entire surface. The chief problem in using modern paints for this technique is that emulsion-type surfaces are much less absorbent than distemper, so there is a tendency for the spots to run. Using thinned colour on a matt emulsion base helps correct this.

OPPOSITE TOP *One of the simplest and yet most effective of decorative tricks with paint, stenkmålning or spatter painting has occupied a special place in Scandinavian interiors for over two hundred years.*

OPPOSITE BELOW *Watery distemper in white and black colour is flicked on to a deep red base colour with the traditional bundle of birch twigs. With a little practice it is possible to vary and control the spatters.*

BELOW LEFT *The black accents are added in an apparently random way, but one which keeps a fairly consistent black spatter going across all the walls.*
BELOW RIGHT *Spatter above the dado is quite often allied to the same technique, but in different colours below. Here the same deep red, plus dark grey, black and a few spots of yellow are spattered onto a pale grey base.*

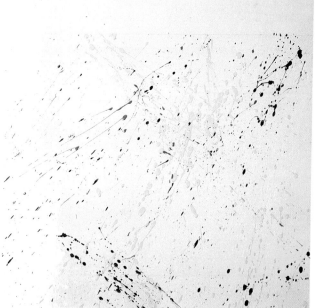

FAUX PORPHYRY

Duskily freckled with colour, obdurately hard to cut and carve, porphyry is a superb decorative stone that somewhat resembles granite taken to a higher power, hard, crisp and glossy, yet soft in colouring. Sweden, historically, was the only European country with natural deposits of porphyry, the other source being the Middle East. Now that Swedish porphyry is no longer quarried – deposits still remain but the cost of extraction is not justified by a keen, but limited, market – old pieces, necessarily simple and classic in shape, are much sought after by collectors. These tend to be small objects such as tazzas, urns, candlesticks and obelisks, though Swedish kings have been interred in porphyry sarcophagi, and the Haga Pavilion boasts one splendid chimneypiece of a gleaming hard-edged perfection that looks as if had been cut yesterday rather than two hundred years ago. As many as 280 different colourations of porphyry are documented, mostly in the pink to brown colour range, but of these a mere twenty were popular, and of those, perhaps three are prime favourites.

As *matières nobles* go, porphyry is an acquired taste, too sombre in colour, too intense, for frivolous or feminine interiors. But just as a touch of black is said by interior decorators to give edge and muscle to a scheme, so a little chink of this mysteriously unyielding material, worked up into a pleasing shape, lends seriousness and virility to any interior. During the eighteenth century it was treated with respect and imagination by leading Scandinavian designers, often combined with ormolu mounts, or crystal drops, for contrast and relief. It is interesting to note that the cutting, as well as quarrying, of Swedish porphyry, was largely undertaken by local seasonal workers, farmers perhaps, who needed a second paying occupation for the winter months when the land was deep in snow. Using primitive lathes and other equipment, they patiently and slowly worked on one of nature's most refractory materials to give the clean, sharp, taut shapes which make old Swedish porphyry so interesting today.

It did not long escape the notice of Scandinavian decorative painters that the mottled, freckled, but mostly predictable patterning of the natural stone was readily imitable in terms of paint. Roger Seamark, who has demonstrated typically Scandinavian paint techniques for this book, is something of a porphyry expert, and his immensely subtle painted imitations of the finer porphyry colourations are in considerable demand today among the cognoscenti of Stockholm. It may require a long apprenticeship to produce the subtler variations on this theme, but faux porphyry is intrinsically a simple spatter technique in which one or two professional 'wrinkles' work to produce an impressive and convincing effect.

Faux porphyry is only another version of Scandinavian spatter painting, but using subtly coordinated colours and more concentrated spattering to simulate one of the 280 colorations of the natural stone. Shown here is a little treasury of faux porphyry from Roger Seamark's studio. The box contains eighteen samples of different porphyry effects from which clients may make a selection. They show how varied the natural colouring is. The lamp base and candlestick have the clean, sharp outlines best suited to this decorative finish. A touch of gilding always sets off faux porphyry handsomely. The tall panel illustrated on the following pages demonstrates the technique.

The porphyry Roger has chosen to demonstrate for this book, is known as Blyberg. It is one of the most popular types, muzzy in effect, pink-red-brown in colouring, a go-with-everything finish, as suited to table tops as to small decorative objects.

The sequence is as follows. A white base coat is first painted over in a red-brown, mars orange and black, as suggested in the colour swatches. When dry this is overglazed, using an oil-based glaze, with Vandyke brown, a transparent but darker shade. Brushed on overall, this is then stippled to even it out, then splashed lightly with turpentine, flicked from a brush, to start a random process of colour separation. Over this, immediately, dirty pink, then grey, is spattered, using a wood chisel to bounce the paint brush off, using oil colours in turpentine. The fact that the basic glaze is still wet, and 'open', encourages the spatter colours to create random but still porphyry effects, as shown in the close-ups. Also, being oil-based paints, a certain transparency remains, helpful

to the final effect, because it suggests depth.

A little practice with the spattering process will soon show how much paint on the brush is needed, and how forcefully the brush should be jogged on the chisel, for a controlled – but not too controlled – effect. Spattering is so easy, manually, that the difficulty is always in knowing when to leave off. A check with our close-up should help.

The final, perfecting, attention is to brush a brown overglaze – more Vandyke brown plus little black or burnt umber – over the whole surface. This is then stippled to even it out, using a 'jabbing' motion with the bristle tips, to remove brushmarks and lend an even patina to the whole. Varnishing is not mandatory, but a mid-sheen effect is what should be aimed at, neither shiny nor flat. This may be best arrived at with full gloss varnish rubbed down finally with fine wire wool, or a soft cloth dipped in rottenstone or pumice powder and a little oil, for lubrication, until the surface is quite slick and smooth, and only faintly glossy.

RIGHT *The dark transparent glaze, tinted with Vandyke brown with a touch of black, is brushed smoothly over the dull red base. While still wet this is flicked lightly with white spirit.*

RIGHT *Pink colour is being spattered onto the board prepared as described above. This is followed by grey spattering.*

OPPOSITE *A close-up of the finished effect based upon the method described here, using a dark transparent glaze over a dull red ground, which is then spattered with pink and grey.*

CASTLES AND PALACES

The great houses of Scandinavia, the mansions, castles and palaces, of which there are a considerable number, were decorated and furnished in the fashionable European style of the time. French influence is particularly noticeable in eighteenth-century interiors and a great deal of decoration was undertaken by foreign painters, or by Scandinavian court painters who had worked or been trained abroad.

However, even the most sophisticated and Francophile interiors have a distinctly Scandinavian look. This is partly created by the mysterious beauty of the pearly light in these northern latitudes; entering low and aslant, it gives the simplest object a luminous sculptural presence, and creates a lyrical chiaroscuro that Scandinavian artists have recreated in their paintings. Also typical of any grand Scandinavian interior are the extraordinary floors: long vistas of bare, scrubbed, blonde planks of noble width and the finest quality. Here, we are rediscovering a common feature of pre-industrial Europe, but to a modern eye the subtle natural colour of the wood offers a pleasurable contrast to showy decoration and fashionable furniture, having rather the same effect as the rush matting used by the interior decorator John Fowler to lighten the interiors of English stately homes.

Monumentality is a feature of Scandinavian castle decoration, long galleries and corridors leading into impressive state rooms. Here, at Skokloster, not far from Stockholm, is one of the long windowed galleries which give onto a central cobbled courtyard. The decoration is grave and impressive, with its baroque-style ceiling decorations, painted dadoes and window embrasures, and

polished slate floor. Skokloster has its decorative sorties, trompe-l'oeil balusters, painted drapery, ceiling beams edged in pastel stripes, like a Neapolitan ice cream, but on the lower floors the impression given is of a certain soldierly austerity as well as subdued magnificence. This is decidedly the home of a famous general and man-of-action rather than a family domicile.

OPPOSITE *Immaculate, elegant, and a touch chilly in its blue and white perfection, this neo-classical interior at Tidö represents the image many people have of an upper-class Scandinavian 'look'. Note the care with which the blue and white theme has been pursued, with blue silk curtains, blue-and-white china and the blue glass bowl to the chandelier. Though sparingly used, the decorative work here is of the highest quality.*

Another characteristic feature of such interiors is an abundant and dashing use of *trompe-l'oeil* finishes. A great deal of what looks at first sight like real marble, plasterwork, hardwood, tortoiseshell, tapestry and stone, turns out on closer examination to be a painted imitation. The delicate pilasters at Svindersvik, the scrumpled drapery behind the boxes in the Court Theatre at Drottningholm, the delicate grisaille-on-gold-leaf work at Gripsholm, the crudely magnificent tortoiseshell and silver-gilt room at Rosenborg in Copenhagen – these are just a few of the painted 'shams' to be found in some of the grandest Scandinavian interiors.

Far from objecting to all this artifice and make-believe, a modern visitor is quite likely to find it more enjoyable than the real thing. Grand houses can be chillingly remote in their ostentation and an atmosphere of conspicuous wealth can have a rather crushing effect. But the Scandinavian castle, with its grisaille and marbling, is immediately engaging. The lavish use of *trompe-l'oeil* may be explained by the fact that, in contrast to other parts of the world, Scandinavia was more dependent on simulated effects. The region was lacking in raw materials and its remoteness meant that imported goods had to travel long distances. It was much easier and more economical to employ a team of painters who could imitate whatever material was required – Italian marble, Brussels tapestry, Lyons silk, Cuban mahogany, Chinese lacquer – rapidly and entertainingly. It is hardly surprising that master painters enjoyed unusual prestige and power in Scandinavian countries.

RIGHT *By the late eighteenth century Scandinavian* trompe-l'oeil *painting at this social level was highly accomplished, as this detail of the impeccable* illusionmålning *at Tidö confirms. The placing of emphasis and of shadows on the trompe mouldings and band of ornament are worth studying by anyone who plans to do similar work.*

ABOVE *Another style of painted ornament popular in the grandest Scandinavian houses was grisaille over gold leaf, to give the effect of carved and moulded plasterwork with parcel gilding. It gives a costly air and dignity to otherwise unembellished surfaces, as in this alcove radiating off the circular salon at Gripsholm which offers spectacular views across Baltic waters. Here the gold leaf decoration gleams as it picks up the slanting northern light.*

Castles

The Scandinavian nobility was numerous, powerful, aggressive and independent right from the days of the sea kings, whose boast it was that only free men manned the oars of their longships. In Viking days they were known at *konung*, or 'men of birth', and when they elected a leader from among themselves, it was without ideas of divine right. When kings failed to do their duty, or their reigns were marred by catastrophe or famine, the nobility not infrequently either killed them or sent them into exile. Against this background, it is not difficult to see why relations between the Scandinavian monarchs and their head-strong barons remained uneasy right down to the nineteenth century.

It was prudent for a noble to build himself a stronghold that could be defended against surprise raids or slow siege. But the shortage of stone was such that for centuries the only two impregnable fortresses in Sweden were the castles at Stockholm and Kalmar. In 1434 when the popular hero Englebrekt Engelbrektsson, a mine-owner from Dalarna, raised his peoples' army and marched on Stockholm, he left a trail of charred ruins. At least twenty-five castles were burned down in this summer of discontent – most of them primitive timber forts easily ignited by hurling red-hot iron balls over the ramparts, or piling up heaps of brushwood outside the walls and smoking the defenders out.

The nobles, it seems, learned the wisdom of building their castles in less flammable materials, such as brick and stone. The many great castles that survive from the late medieval period are usually built of stone rather than brick, although where brick was used, remaining vestiges of external paintwork suggest that the brick was limewashed and then 'quarried', that is painted in iron-oxide red to imitate dressed stone courses. (This method of upgrading brick fortresses was not confined to Scandinavia: the White Tower of the Tower of London got its name from the colour of its limewash finish.)

Inside the stone castles, the walls were treated in a similar way (we know from The Book of Rolls that Henry III of England ordered the whitewashed interiors in his palaces to be quarried in red). To a modern eye that regards stone as sufficiently handsome unadorned, this may sound garish, but remaining examples – found in castles such as Gripsholm as well as in small churches – show that the effect was highly decorative, especially when the red was further used to doodle ornament round windows and doorways in imitation of carved ornament. This style of *trompe-l'oeil* decoration was not intended to deceive but, like the green walls spangled with gold stars which were another of Henry III's favourite schemes, it expressed the medieval love of colour and display.

OPPOSITE *A very different period atmosphere emanates from Gripsholm interiors on the ground floor of the former Royal palace. The High Renaissance atmosphere of this part of the building, with its massively thick walls and light filtering in wanly through deep embrasures, as here, was recreated in the late nineteenth century by a scheme of wall painting, in muted colours and a wide variety of motifs researched and assembled from all over Sweden. The effect, as of walls wrapped in faded embroidery, is subtle and picturesque.*

ABOVE *A detail from the adjacent Queen's Chamber shows an interesting variation on the chequered theme. Here there is a deliberate use of optical illusion which may have been inspired by a style of brickwork fashionable at this period in Denmark.*

OPPOSITE *Something of the heraldic splendour of an authentic early sixteenth-century decorated interior comes across in this view of the King's Chamber at Denmark's Nyborg Slott with its simple but dramatic scheme of monochrome chequers contrasted with a ceiling distempered a soft red, and floor tiles of simple glazed earthenware. Note how the chequers change size and rhythm as they emphasize the window arch. This floor at Nyborg was added on to the medieval fortress in 1500, and the decoration dates from shortly after that. The furnishings shown are contemporaneous, though not original to Nyborg.*

Most Scandinavian castles are 'water castles', built on the shores of the sea or of lakes so that, when their moats are filled with water, they crouch in all their impressive bulk on what are virtually offshore islands. The mass of these fortresses, punctuated by their imposing turrets and seen against a flat, indeterminate shoreline, creates a brooding sense of power. Kronborg, Frederiksborg, Gripsholm, Sjöo and Läckö are arrogant strongholds bristling with defiance.

However, the most striking late medieval castle interior that has survived is to be found in Nyborg Slott, on the Danish island of Fyn. This small brick castle is all that remains of the imposing fortress where Danish kings and their nobility assembled for Councils of State. The astonishing interiors are all on the first floor, and were added on to the twelfth-century fortress in 1500. Originally this upper floor was reached by external wooden stairs leading on to a wooden gallery overlooking the courtyard. Today a spiral staircase in a small turret leads directly into the King's Chamber. Like the Queen's Chamber, which opens directly out of it, the walls of this towering space are entirely covered with a regularly repeating chequered pattern painted in white, grey and black. Unusually for the period, perhaps, the only colour is on the ceiling, whose massive wooden beams are distempered in a soft red of an almost velvety texture. The floor is also a dull red, paved with uneven clay tiles an inch thick.

The chequered pattern in the King's Chamber, which continues without a break over the hooded fireplace, and gives way to larger variations on the window arches, is a straightforward geometric design of squares divided into four triangles, one white, one black and two grey. Next door in the Queen's Chamber the wall painting, still in monochrome, is an exercise in a rudimentary form of *trompe-l'oeil*, where a flat wall surface is painted to suggest that it is made up of piled-up blocks set at an angle, so that the corners face into the room. The inspiration for this was probably a form of decorative brickwork used in southern Scandinavia at this time, which was known as *opus spicatus*, or 'spiky work'. Renaissance builders, later, were to be fond of interpreting this design in marble paving, giving a disconcerting three-dimensional effect, and such was the perennial appeal of the simple but effective device that it became absorbed into the European needlework tradition in the popular pieced design known as 'building blocks'.

LEFT *Neither the colours nor the shapes are too precise or even, as can be seen from this close-up of the original painting in the King's Chamber. Timbers incorporated into the walls of these two splendid apartments have been painted in with the wall chequers, though not plastered over.*

ABOVE *One of the prettier decorative inventions of the period, this slender husk-and-garland motif has a lively, refreshing dynamism. Note too the fine quality of water gilding on the small mirror.*

OPPOSITE *A brilliantly simple and effective variant on the 'faux' panel idea in one of the tiny, low-ceilinged garret suites at Gripsholm where courtiers and ladies-in-waiting were accommodated in the eighteenth century. The panel effect is painted on canvas wall-hangings, the white panels inset into a grey-blue frame, the arrowy whorls painted in the same sort of grey-blue, the mouldings gilt and then overpainted. Note how the panel treatment continues over the jib door to a built-in closet, also the simple coving at ceiling level.*

The chequered interiors at Nyborg provide the visitor with a vivid sense of the richness of medieval decoration. Almost bare of furnishings, as they now are, these remarkable apartments are still impressive. When the Danish royal family used them, and the walls were hung with banners and embroideries, and the fireplace held blazing logs, they must have been truly magnificent. Much of the attractiveness of what is a simple decorative idea used on a grand scale, is due to the subtle texture of the traditional distemper paints.

In the Swedish castle of Gripsholm, by Lake Mälaren, one plunges immediately into romantic gloom, the oblique northern light reduced to shadowy chiaroscuro by windows set back in deep embrasures in the thickness of the massive walls. Gripsholm, as it stands today, was built by Gustavus I Vasa in 1537. Inside this commanding fortress, the dusky chambers are rich with colour in the form of painted decoration and stamped and gilded leather hangings, which are illuminated here and there by the thin light let in by the old, faintly tinted glass in the deep window bays. The walls were redecorated in the late nineteenth century in the style of late medieval/Renaissance wall paintings. Admirably executed in now faded colours, the delicate floral and geometric ornaments enrich the dim old apartments as gently as faded embroideries.

The special delight of Gripsholm is one peculiar to huge, old Scandinavian castles and palaces and, paradoxically, is a triumph of the miniature. The upper floors and the garrets of these venerable piles are an enchanting rookery of diminutive suites of rooms set aside for the gentlemen- and ladies-in-waiting attached to various royal personages. At Gripsholm, the decoration in these doll's-house interiors belongs to a later date than the grand state apartments. Most of them are Gustavian in style, the walls hung with painted canvas *tapeter* and discreetly embellished with *trompe-l'oeil* frames, incorporating flowers, ribbons and strings of pearls, or classical motifs such as ribboned husks or reeds. The furnishings are sparse, but elegant: a pretty carved mirror; a pair of Gustavian chairs, either *ax stol*, with carved wooden backs and straight legs, or the French-influenced *ros stol*, with upholstered backs. These small, simple, but refined rooms are dominated by bed and stove, both of which seem to be crammed in beneath the Wendy-house ceilings. Beds belong either to the alcove type, in its most aristocratic form, or the draped type in its most vivacious Scandinavian style, with curtains and canopy of simple checked cotton or linen in pink, blue or green and white. If one had to collect the essential ingredients of a characteristic Scandinavian style, they would be found here and would include a towering faience stove, pastel-coloured *tapeter*, bare floorboards, and a milkmaid of a bed recessed into an alcove and draped in checked cotton with a pair of *ax stol* with matching dust covers placed either side of it.

ABOVE *Check, gilt, rococo flower borders and a* trompe-l'oeil *dado add up to a quintessentially Swedish vignette.*

RIGHT *Demure doll's-house charm could hardly go further than in this adorable little room at Gripsholm, designated for the Queen's principal lady-in-waiting in the eighteenth century. Panel effects in here are painted directly on plastered walls, rather than on canvas, and there is no cornice. This is said to be the first room in Sweden where checked linen was elevated from being used merely for dust covers to become a pretty as well as practical furnishing fabric in its own right. Checked bed-hangings in various colourways, always with white, turn up over and over again in Swedish houses of any pretensions, almost always teamed up with chairs covered or cushioned in matching fabric. It is the confident simplicity of such ideas that makes Scandinavian decoration of this period so interesting to modern interior designers. They remain entirely workable today.*

OPPOSITE *Even with so many bare patches where paintings once hung, enough remains of the original decoration of the Hall of Chivalry at Läckö to show why this colourful but disciplined scheme of decoration proved so influential in Sweden during the Scandinavian baroque period. Complete, and furnished with the extravagance for which de la Gardie was notorious, it must have been a magnificent space. The decorating is a triumph of trompe-l'oeil executed in grisaille; it is important to be clear when looking at this photograph that both ceiling and walls are in fact perfectly flat, and all the lavish carved moulding and deep ceiling compartments are pure illusion. What makes the grisaille especially striking is the use of a deep red background colour, a combination that was to find many imitators. Though to paint a room of this size so elaborately must have been costly in man hours, there can be no doubt that the illusion was cheaper than the real thing. It was also, given the remoteness of central Sweden and a shortage of specialist craftsmen, much simpler to set a team of painters to work simulating grand effects and noble materials. The dangling putti are a curious addition, perhaps intended to enliven the flatness of the painted ceiling.*

The most influential great house of the seventeenth century was Läckö, the medieval castle on Lake Vattern which had been given in 1617 by Gustavus II Adolphus to one of his generals, Jakob de la Gardie, as a reward for distinguished service in the Russian wars. Jakob's son Magnus de la Gardie, who inherited Läckö in 1652, became the favourite of Queen Christina. Magnus was proud and extravagant: his Stockholm palace was christened 'Makalos' or 'Matchless' in imitation of Henry Tudor's Nonesuch. At Läckö he set about a programme of improvements and grandiose decorations designed to make it 'matchless' among the rural castles of Sweden. He employed German builders (Franz Stimer and Mathias Han) and the Swedish painters Johan Werner and Johan Hammer. They worked for over twenty years at Läckö under de la Gardie's direction, and created painted interiors of great magnificence and lavishness for the state apartments. De la Gardie must have been an inspiring as well as exacting patron. The Hall of Chivalry, in particular, is a masterpiece, a great medieval space to which de la Gardie's team added the drama and colour of rich surface decoration in the heroic style. The ceilings are painted to resemble plaster, with grey-blue toned grisaille work on a deep red ground reaching its most sumptuous expression. Groups of trophies cover the immense compartmented ceiling, swirling acanthus motifs fill panels outlined in *trompe-l'oeil* mouldings, and great pendants of painted fruit and flowers are crammed into the narrowest of wall spaces. There is not a simple bolection moulding that does not sport a narrow gilt fillet and intense grisaille decoration simulating carving. And yet, with its rich red ground tone subdued by so much monochromatic decoration, the overall effect is noble and dignified, sufficiently accomplished to rank with the greatest continental interiors of the seventeenth century, and virile enough to carry off a swarm of carved and painted cherubs suspended from its ceiling without for a moment putting one in mind of a boudoir. It is hardly surprising that the decoration at Läckö, and of this hall in particular, took de la Gardie's compatriots by storm. Some of the effects seen here were recreated in a much more modest way; in a few decades hardly a boarded ceiling above peasant level did not sport a grisaille wreath or oval in grey blue on a deep red ground. A century later, the idea had become assimilated into the vernacular style and de la Gardie's martial decorations had been transformed into a pattern of four rosettes, or a single outsize one, boldly if awkwardly rendered on a whitewashed plank ceiling.

All building work at Läckö ceased in 1680, when Karl XI, who sought to break the power of the nobles, repossessed much of their lands and property. De la Gardie lost most of his possessions to the Crown and, although he kept Läckö, it passed after his death into other hands.

ABOVE *Skokloster Castle: a detail from a painted ceiling on the top floor showing a small painting of the castle itself surrounded by scrolls and blooms.*

The castle of Skokloster on the shores of Lake Mälaren is a splendid example of Swedish post-Renaissance on a large scale. This dramatic whitewashed and black-capped fortress was designed by the German architect Caspar Vogel for Carl Gustav Wrangel, General-in-Chief of the army under Queen Christina, as summer home for his family of eleven children (six of whom – all boys – died in childhood). Portraits of the children, stiff, unwinking mannikins in the style of the age, hang in a solemn row alongside their parents, framed in silver leaf striped with grass green. The walls behind them are covered with the stamped, painted and gilded leather that was the acme of splendour in its day and which was applied to walls throughout the castle as freely as we would use wallpaper. Now tarnished to a dark, subdued richness, when newly hung (as one can ascertain by looking behind the portraits) it was as gaudy as the coloured foil of chocolate wrappings.

Wrangel was a man of war, rather than a patron of the arts, but he was fond of acquiring other people's property as the legitimate spoils of war. After the capture of Leipzig, he wrote to his father from the battlefield: 'The archduke's baggage and plate are among the booty. I have obtained his carriage and gold service.' Skokloster contains the strangest assortment of period furnishings, some of it remarkable, some of it in doubtful taste; what is exceptional is the castle's rich collection of *bonad* or wall-hangings. Modern taste might be forgiven, perhaps, for finding the humblest of these, the so-called Fransk or French *tapeter*, the most appealing. Woven of linen and wool in prettily coloured stripes, these were destined to be hung in the servants' rooms.

Ascending through the five storeys of this immense building, another use of painted decoration manifests itself. Vigorous, if crude, painted drapery festoons the lower part of simply whitewashed walls in a manner reminiscent of medieval Tuscan interiors, and the same influence may perhaps be traced in the gaily decorated ceiling beams. In the long passages, ceiling treatment is of the simplest; whitewashed beams are edged with alternating borders of pale blue, pink, yellow. The most decorative and flowery treatment, with flowers and leaves twined the length of painted beams, is to be found, incongruously enough, in the weapon-hung chamber which once formed Wrangel's private armoury.

OPPOSITE *The library on the top floor of Skokloster has a fascinating and unusual medley of decorative elements, painted drapery, floral swags, whitewashed beams banded in colours and spotted with outsize blooms. The effect is charming but oddly frivolous for the library of a famous military man.*

The long gallery which leads into the blue-and-white drawing-room at Tidö has been recently re-marbled in the original colours, golden sienna and a grey/blue/green in the Kalmard style. The colours make a handsome background to an unusually fine collection of paintings and sculpture, and two monumental stoves. The quality of all the detailing at Tidö is remarkable, even in Scandinavia where such small items as door handles and finger plates are often beautifully designed and made.

ABOVE *The high standard of latter-day marbling in Sweden can be gauged from this corner of the repainted gallery. It is interesting to note that the diagonal movement so typical of provincial marbling is also used here, though the technique is infinitely more skilled and sophisticated.*

The French influence that gradually predominates in the architecture of great houses in Sweden during the seventeenth century, reaching its apogee in the eighteenth century, can be largely traced to the influence of the French architect, Simon de la Vallée, who first came to Sweden at the invitation of the powerful Oxenstierna family in 1637. He built three castles for the family, of which the most famous is Tidö, in Vastmanland. In the logic and symmetry of its ground plan, and the suppression of medieval features like turrets and towers in favour of a classically inspired simplicity relieved by sparing ornament, Tidö provided a model that was much imitated. The interiors at Tidö are of comparable elegance, formal and French in style, impeccably carried out, and without the rusticity (the floors for instance are polished, not scrubbed) that one associates with great houses in the Scandinavian manner. The hallway has been marbled throughout in the last few years; this is conventional *illusionmålning* of a high standard, though perhaps a shade or two more vivid than the usual Siena marbling treatment. The boiseries here are real, rather than painted simulation. This is a country palace of great distinction architecturally and it is richly and magnificently furnished, but apart from the superb tiled stoves and a prevalence of painted Gustavian chairs in white touched with gold leaf, it is not characteristically Scandinavian in feel.

RIGHT *Another detail from the blue-and-white drawing room showing the superb faience stove, and a pair of slender candle sconces, as well as interesting pelmet-style window drapery.*

This is a section of painted cornice which, with the painted doors shown opposite, is all that remains of the seventeenth-century tower rooms at Sjöo castle, outside Stockholm. Even in Sweden grisaille decoration of such crispness and elaboration is rare. Strictly speaking this is monochrome rather than grisaille, since the decoration is carried out in tones of buff and sepia on a drab green background. Probably the walls below were hung with canvas painted in the manner of verdure tapestry, a colour scheme which would have harmonized well.

A peculiarity of Scandinavian architecture, and of Swedish architecture in particular, is the way the most famous practitioners belonged to dynasties. Simon de la Vallée was followed by his son, Jean de la Vallée, while Nicodemus Tessin the Elder was succeeded by Nicodemus the Younger and eventually by Carl Gustav Tessin, Royal tutor, ambassador to Versailles and sometime architect too.

Nicodemus Tessin the Elder built Sjöo in Uppland, and is supposed to have worked on Skokloster, for Carl Gustav Wrangel. Sjöo is a more advanced and fashionable building than Skokloster; its internal plan was modelled on the royal palace of Drottningholm, which was designed as a series of symmetrically arranged apartments linked by a central staircase and vestibule in the French manner. Internally, Sjöo shares many of the decorative features of Skokloster, such as magnificent baroque ceiling decoration, much grisaille work on doors, and on brightly painted decorative panels under the windows. It would be interesting to know who carried out the painting here, because it is of an

exceptional standard, the coved ceiling painted in grisaille against a green background being especially handsome. This is a superb example of *trompe-l'oeil* painting, managing to be delicate and realistic in its shading and detail without loss of spirit and authority.

Although Sjöo may represent an advance in compactness and clarity of plan over Skokloster, it was in most respects just the solid, old-fashioned, sort of building Tessin's clients preferred. The cultural time-lag so noticeable in Scandinavian architecture and decoration was, at least partly, an expression of the innate conservatism of clients, rather than the result of being out of touch with the fashionable European ideas. When the Tessins travelled in search of ideas, and models, for future commissions, it was invariably buildings of an earlier, already unfashionable, period that they chose to study and imitate. The attitude seemed to have been that what was good enough for the client's father, and his father before him, was good enough for the client too.

Sjöo Castle: the same monochrome colours and style of acanthus scroll is used on the door panels in the tower rooms, but here the background is gold leaf, giving a sumptuously warm effect.

Rococo Painted Panelling

From the mid-eighteenth century it became fashionable in Scandinavia, for almost a hundred years, to divide walls into two main fields bisected by a dado, real or painted, running round at chair-back height. In the tiny low-ceilinged rooms on attic floors of grand houses such as the Haga Pavilion and Gripsholm, the dado may be much lower, a foot or so above the skirting. All this was in accordance with European fashion, though a decade or two behind as was usually the case in Scandinavia. But where Scandinavian practice differed from the rest was in the almost universal choice of painted canvas or linen to fill in the upper wall surface above the dado, instead of the rich silks, brocades, Chinese wallpapers, lacquered panels, and other inventions popular on the Continent, and in England. What other countries achieved with sumptuous fabrics, or carved and painted or gilded boiseries, the Scandinavian painters customarily suggested with paint. At first their sleight of hand was confined to embellishing canvas panels in a wooden framework (as at Ekolssund); but as the fashion spread to lesser houses, or the lesser rooms of great houses, the whole panelled effect began to be implied with paint, to the point where large wall surfaces would be simply divided into suitably scaled and proportioned 'panels' by means of painted fillets, faux mouldings, or decorated bands. These were then usually given a more graceful appearance by loops of flowers, or twirling ribbons, or strings of pearls, caught up by a bow or a gilt ring or some other device in mid-panel.

Perhaps this style of decoration was once prevalent in other European countries too, but where the Scandinavian countries stand out uniquely is in the sheer quantity of original effects that survive, and the variety of decorative ideas that they incorporate. The interest of these to a modern reader must be that they provide a rich field of reference to anyone, professional decorator or ambitious amateur, who is looking for a fairly easy and inexpensive device for adding structure, colour, and emphasis to characterless or featureless rooms. Painted directly onto walls, rather than canvas, these simple but nicely judged decorative flourishes give a remarkably finished air for a modest expenditure of time and money. The humblest examples are often the most attractive: the simplest outlined moulding in a contrasting colour, or the prettily detailed bands used in some of the tiny attics of the Haga Pavilion, attics in which the painted effects also substitutes for cornices and skirting details.

This book is full of examples of such devices, but to encourage readers to copy them, some characteristic mid- to late eighteenth-century ideas are reproduced here, from the first pencil outline to the finished 'panel'.

The most difficult part is arriving at a convincing module for the sub-division of the walls. Small, regularly repeating panels are easier to handle but belong more to wallpapers than to painted schemes of this sort. Usually a Scandinavian room will combine large panels with small ones, aiming at symmetry where possible. Thus panels either side of a central stove, could be identical, but there might be a larger panel on the shorter wall, with small overdoor panels to complete the scheme. Study the various examples shown before deciding. It is obviously helpful to draw the walls out to scale and try different effects on them with coloured felt pens, but sometimes instinct is just as reliable a guide. However, once painted and 'located' by furniture and pictures, such applied decoration always seems to look right and convincing.

In our examples a soft conte pencil was used to rough in the rectangular 'panel' outlines, plus the various decorative additions in the way of bows, bamboo, leaves and so on. The wall surface was first finished in white standard emulsion (but it could be any colour, or a different paint, bearing in mind that final overglazing will modify the overall tone) and the outlines pencilled in lightly using the usual painters' aids: plumb bob (a heavy object tied to a length of string can substitute), steel rule and spirit level, to obtain accurate verticals and horizontals. In a complete room all these outlines would be placed before starting to paint.

Rococo bamboo

This more fanciful treatment is in the rococo spirit, the sort of design Lars Bolander might have used for a smaller room than the many he decorated at Ekolssund and Stuerefors. The bamboo was first painted in ochre, then heightened with white and black as shown, using a fine brush. The sprays of leaves were then painted with a fine brush in dark green, but with occasional paler highlights. The ensemble was overglazed in a burnt umber shade, quite liberally, to create a deep cream colour, but then the bamboo highlights were wiped out with a clean cloth to bring them up.

All these decorations were painted in acrylic colours for speedy drying, but they would originally have been painted either in oil colours or in egg-oil tempera, the favoured medium with clients because of its ultimate rock-hard durability (tempera cannot be removed with a blow torch) but not with painters, since its drying time is lengthy, especially in a cold climate.

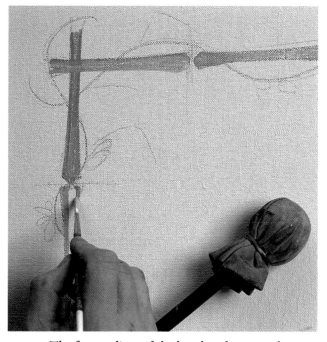

ABOVE *The first outlines of the bamboo framework.*
BELOW *The finished effect in close-up.*

ABOVE *Rapid flicks of green add pointed leaves.*
BELOW *Bamboo panel decoration on a larger scale.*

Neo-classical leaves and loops

This simple but effective treatment shows the effectiveness of highlights. A plain blue fillet, and yellow ochre rings, strongly underlined in white, gain a three-dimensional presence, with the ochre remarkably resembling gilding at first glance. The leafy garlands here are more carefully differentiated than in the previous example, the leaves larger, more shaded and variegated, but remaining graceful and expressive rather than botanically exact. Again, overglazing in a milder tone pulls the treatment together, and gives a suggestion of age, effective for creating atmosphere in blank new surroundings.

Slender blue moulding with gilt rings provides the framework for trailing ivy in the neo-classical style example of faux panelling shown here. Note how roughly the blue is laid on, in expectation of further lighter and darker lines. Yellow, usually ochre, was traditionally used to suggest gold leaf.

Again fine stemwork variegated with clusters of leaves, makes a suitably delicate garland to loop from ring to ring across the blue 'panel'.

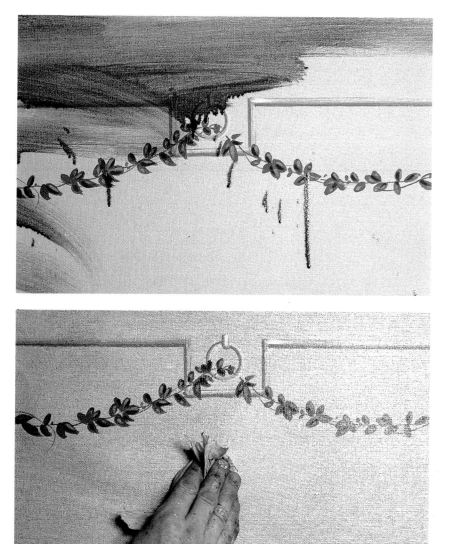

A dark muddy coloured overglaze is wiped on to soften the background white and blend all the decoration together.

A soft cheesecloth or lint-free rag is used to even up and blend the overglaze so that it looks natural, like an antique patina.

The final effect of this 'faux panel' design, once it has been overglazed.

Neo-classical bow and husks

A feminine, bedroom, boudoir, bathroom type of design featuring the ever-popular three-petalled bow with curly ends, and the classical husk and pearl ornament on the decorative loops which are a feature of painted eighteenth-century decoration everywhere in Europe. The first picture shows them being filled in with Prussian blue somewhat crudely but exactly. White then highlights and models the husks and pearls and, carefully applied in close vertical stripes, converts a rough bow into a gleaming ribbon. A little dark blue applied with a fine brush makes the bow shapes more emphatic. Finally the whole motif is overglazed, in a greyer shade this time, to soften and antique it pleasantly.

Whether or not this type of painted decoration should be given a protective coat of varnish must depend on the place where it is, and the amount of wear it is likely to get. Varnish a bathroom, using dead flat clear varnish, but a bedroom may not need this last attention.

OPPOSITE TOP *Foundation strokes, in mid-blue, for the bow and husks treatment over a slim blue framework which together make up another attractive neo-classical style of decoration. These strokes are brushed in roughly, because there are more to follow.*

OPPOSITE BELOW *Highlights in pure white together with fine brushwork in dark blue have given the gleam of silk moire to the stylized clover leaf bow plus modelling to the strings of 'husks'.*

BELOW *The completed design showing the softened effect of overglazing. A 'panel' like this would usually be set in a framework painted in another colour. Thus, here, the outer framework would be a blue like the mid-tone used in the decoration, or possibly a grey darker than the background tone of the panel.*

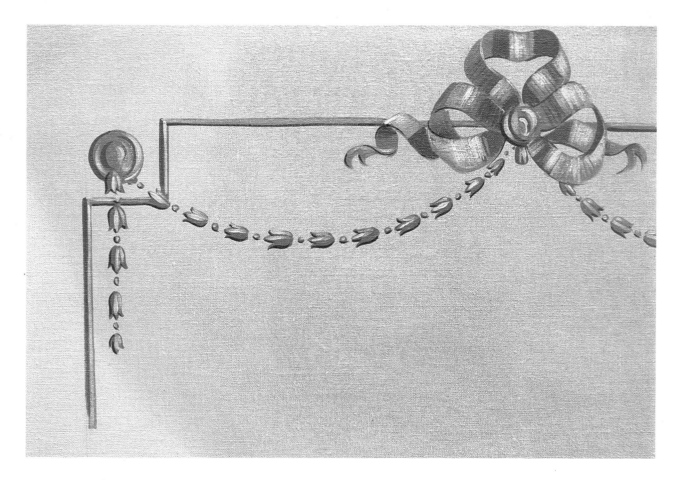

GRISAILLE

The term 'grisaille' comes from the French 'gris', or grey, and is applied to a *trompe-l'oeil* technique used to imitate bas-relief carving, usually in tones of grey, though tones of brown, green or blue may also be used in different contexts. It was much used in decorating Italian Renaissance interiors, and came back into favour in the eighteenth-century neo-classical period. It is still a popular effect with designers and painters looking for a subdued style of painted ornament which will give a dignified effect without conflicting with other decorative elements in a room. One often finds grisaille used in overdoor panels, as a frieze, or to suggest niches filled with statuary, or panels of bas relief carving.

The Scandinavian, or more properly, Swedish, use of grisaille is rather different from the rest of Europe in that it was more often used to suggest carved or cast plaster decoration, and was most often used on ceilings, though it also appears on wall panels, door panels, covings and cornices. In addition, this type of grisaille was often combined with touches of strong colour, red, blue, and sometimes gold. Though there are exquisitely skilful examples of grisaille in the neo-classical vein, often applied over gold leaf, to be seen in the grandest Scandinavian interiors, like the Haga Pavilion and Gripsholm, more often the approach is boldly decorative rather than cunningly deceptive. Applied, as the grisaille ceiling treatments often are, directly onto whitewashed boards, the intention can never have been seriously to fool the eye; what was aimed at, and successfully achieved, was a richness of ornament above to balance and complement painted *tapeter*, or stamped gilt leather hangings, on the walls. These splendid grisaille ceiling treatments are one of the many surprises which traditional Scandinavian painted interiors have to offer. It is perhaps surprising that they have not been more widely imitated throughout Europe. It seems likely that the ceiling patterns, invariably symmetrical, and usually compartmented, were imitated from early engravings of decorated plasterwork ceilings of the sort architects like Inigo Jones devised for their clients, and which would have circulated in Europe during the seventeenth century.

Grisaille panel

A typically Scandinavian use of grisaille, boldly defined on a coloured ground, is demonstrated here on a smaller than ceiling scale, on the sort of panel which was often used in important buildings during the seventeenth century and early eighteenth century to fill in and dramatize the wall space below a window, as at Skokloster. The intention in this case might have been to suggest either carved plasterwork, or carved and painted wooden panels. One can imagine a similar motif, scaled up or down, in a modern context, making striking decorative panels on an old cupboard, or chest, or even on doors and shutters with fielded panels. Mouldings are not strictly necessary, as our example shows, since these can readily be suggested in grisaille on a completely flat surface following the system shown.

The paints used here were acrylic based, for speed of drying and coverage, but standard undercoat, which has a lean 'old' consistency, or of course linseed-oil paint, are options. Another useful paint, for anyone wanting a brown-red base, could be red oxide primer, with a little burnt umber and/or mars orange oil coloured mixed in.

Three stages in the creation of bold grisaille acanthus leaf scrolls, of the sort seen on panels at Skokloster and Läckö, and on countless Scandinavian ceilings and cupboards. Here they are painted on a deep red ground, as they tended to be shown during the baroque period, for warmth and richness as well as contrast. Grisaille work is usually in shades of grey, as here, but can turn up in other monochromatic treatments, such as the example from Sjöo castle on page 134.

A plumb line and spirit level were used to draw out the rectangle outline of the panel in pencil. Then, on the dry base colour, the boldly curving anthemion type foliage was roughed in first with white chalk, then brushed in with white paint using a flat sable brush in size 10 or 8, and working enough paint into the bristles to complete a stroke each time. As with *rosmålning*, which uses almost identical brushstrokes, the idea is to arrive at a confident, relaxed but controlled rhythm. It helps to practise the curving teardrop shapes, in different sizes, on a board or spare piece of paper first.

Using a mid-grey paint, the white shapes were now shaded with finer grey strokes as shown to suggest three-dimensional modelling. These will tend to fall most heavily to one side of the motif, as if the light were casting a shadow there, but, as our example shows, this will need balancing up here and there on the other side and through the centre. The grey was then darkened in patches with a fine sable pencil and dark grey paint, keeping the dark shading sparing, and fine.

The next stage was to paint the outline to each panel and the *trompe-l'oeil* framework, including a 'trompe' moulding above at dado level. Using a marlstick – the professional's aid to painting straight lines steadily – the red panel was outlined in black, a half-inch wide, all round. This was then highlighted in white, as shown. When the paint had dried, masking tape was stuck down over the outlining, to protect it from overpainting, while the intervening areas were painted in mid-grey paint. The dado side is twice as wide as the rest, to allow for a trompe moulding. When the mid-grey paint was dry, masking tape was stuck down, a thick and a thin strip, on the dado, as shown. The entire pale grey was then dragged over with a brownish-black glaze, imitating the joints of a real wood frame. The tapes were peeled off leaving paler lines remaining on the dado side to represent the prominent parts of the moulding. A white line makes them stand further forward, while a little more dark overglaze strengthens the shadows. With a very fine brush and black paint, 'joints' in the panel frame were drawn in, together with tiny circles to suggest period pegged construction.

The last touch was a dark overglaze over the grisaille work and red ground, to soften and knit together the ensemble. This can be brushed on quite thickly and then stippled to smooth it in the darker areas, or wiped off with a rag where highlights are needed. Or, if an evenly toned glaze is required, it can be evened up by gentle rubbing with a soft rag.

As a rule the larger the scale the cruder the technique, though there was a tendency for all decorative work, grisaille included, to become more refined during the eighteenth century, culminating in the spectacularly sophisticated decoration, on gold leaf, in the Haga *salle des glaces*.

ABOVE *Masking tape outlines the area of the deep red panel. A 'mouse' or plumb line ensures true verticals. The acanthus scroll shapes are lightly sketched in with conte pencil.*

ABOVE *A fat brush and dark grey/brown is used to shade a* trompe *moulding on the simulated framework or dado.*

ABOVE *A soft pointed brush blocks in the petal shapes in white. Again, this is the rough framework, so it does not have to be precise or complete.*

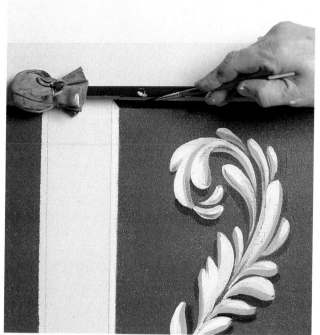

ABOVE *Steadied by a marlstick, a chisel-ended brush is used to add a narrow outline in dark grey on two sides of the grisaille panel.*

ABOVE *White highlights are added with a slim brush to strengthen the* trompe-l'oeil *moulding effect.*

ABOVE *Overglazing in a dark colour simulates the patina of age and blends the ensemble together. Any highlights which may be wanted can be wiped out with a cloth.*

STATELY HOMES

Though there are Scandinavian stately homes from all periods, and in many styles, the characteristic façade glimpsed up an avenue of limes between handsome wrought-iron gates is an eighteenth-century one, long and low, often with neo-classical detailing like applied pilasters, painted a creamy-ochre. Often a pair of small detached wings, or pavilions, stand either side of the forecourt. Viewed against a frieze of dark trees, the effect is glamorously blonde in a cool, reserved way. Scandinavian domestic architecture, even at this aristocratic level, is not where one expects to find monumental or theatrical effects. Gardens are less important than they would be in an equivalent English setting; often the surrounding pastureland merges into a sort of wild garden, though close to the house there may be a suggestion of formality with clipped box and yews and regularly disposed urns. One charming feature of older gardens, such as Sandemar, or the Norwegian Damsgard Have, is a line of small wooden figures, painted white and carved in the manner of ships' figureheads, standing on low plinths. These were obviously intended to give something of the consequential air of marble statuary set in formal gardens, but because of their size – they are barely three feet high – and the endearingly rustic quality of the carving, they resemble an upper-class family of garden gnomes, or perhaps, trolls. They are also something of a nuisance; being vulnerable to damp and cold they have all to be brought indoors before winter.

By the same de Saly who sculpted a splendid equestrian bronze in the centre of Amalienborg square, this dashing portrait bust in glazed white ceramic is one of a pair decorating the pale grey salon at Marienlyst Slott, north of Copenhagen. The restraint of the decor at Marienlyst seems typically Danish; pastel shades relieved with white are a frequent choice.

Neo-classical motifs in gold leaf and colour on a pale grey and white background create a cool, calm effect in the dining room at Bjorkssund, a beautifully decorated and furnished eighteenth-century great house south of Stockholm. The leather-covered chairs are in reindeer hide.

These aristocratic country residences would usually have had their town counterpart, a more architecturally sophisticated mansion built round a courtyard rather in the manner of a Parisian *hôtel privé*. Whereas many country houses remain in private hands, few of these town mansions are privately owned today. The mansion of the Fersen family (Count Fersen was the coachman on the French royal family's disastrous flight to Vincennes) in the centre of Stockholm, is now a bank; Frederiksborg Slott in Copenhagen, which overlooks a beautifully landscaped park, has become a military academy. Dehn Palœ, the austerely handsome private palace built in the mid-eighteenth century for a Danish privy counsellor, just round the corner from the Amalienborg Palace, is now the headquarters of the Danish Pharmacists' Association. These days stately home owners probably live in their country estates more than they used to. Many of them try to combine the farming of their estates with a job, to which they commute, in the city.

If the representative exterior of the typical stately home is modestly neo-classical in style, the Danish or Swedish interior aspires towards the refined elegance we tend to think of as French. In contrast to the virility of the seventeenth-century 'baroque' style, with its dark, dignified colours and massively architectural detailing, these late eighteenth-century interiors are sparklingly feminine, airy, flowery and full of light. The light streams in through tall windows, reflects back from pier-glasses and is scattered in bursts of brilliance from chandeliers, girandoles and exquisitely pretty wall-sconces, set with mirrors and looped with crystal drops. (Scandinavian glass chandeliers have a distinctive and easily recognized character.) Rooms appear lighter partly because ceilings are loftier (at least in the newly built rooms of the period) but also because they are no longer laden with the painted grisaille wreaths and compartments of the baroque period; mostly they are quite plain (usually boarded in the more rustic *slott*) and painted white, with maybe a delicate cornice touched with gold leaf. Occasionally, as at Svindersvik, a 'sky' ceiling was painted in pale blue with delicate clouds, another fashionable eighteenth-century device. The architectural detail in these rooms is newly delicate, in the style of French boiseries, and forms, in its ubiquitous pearl-grey paint, a quiet background to that new focus of decorative interest, the walls.

Walls are now treated differently, sub-divided according to the classical orders with a dado running round at chair rail height. Below the dado is panelling (or a painted simulation) and above it painted canvas or linen hangings are stretched and nailed to cover the space up to the ceiling. This combination of panelled dado and stretched fabric was one that had gradually become fashionable in European interiors, though the French and English tended to use lavish silk, or brocade, or handpainted wallpaper, pasted onto canvas, above the dado. In Scandinavia decoratively painted *tapeter* were almost unanimously preferred, possibly because they were cheaper and lasted longer, possibly because there were now many more master painters, whose skill had been improved by study in European capitals, to fill these new spaces with imaginative decorative schemes. The brilliant and cultured Gustav III of Sweden, as a young man, had shown what could be done

An exceptionally pretty and elegant
example of eighteenth-century
tapeter *painting on canvas, also from
Bjorkssund. All the smaller panels
contain their* trompe-l'oeil *gilt oval
frames hanging from painted bows
like outsize lockets. The delicate
candy stripes are hand painted; the
painted border to the striped panels,
with its bright blue feather curling
round a slender rod, is exquisitely
done. Note the stone surround to the
wooden floor.*

149

French influence is apparent in this rather feminine and flowery drawing room at Ekolssund, in Sweden, with its boiseries painted grey and gilded in the French manner. Parquet floors are an innovation of this period which reinforce the intended look of a French château; though handsome, they always look out of place in this country of bleached pine boards. In their day they were at once fashionable, different and a status symbol. The painted decoration is by Lars Bolander, one of the most skilful of eighteenth-century Swedish decorative painters.

ABOVE *Beribboned melons, and other exotica including fruit that might be lychees or loganberries, make a colourful centrepiece for borders on a wall panel.*

with the accomplished interiors painted at what was then his summer residence, Ekolssund, by the Swedish painter Lars Bolander. In the large and elegant salon, Bolander has painted brilliantly colourful borders of exotic fruit, flowers and birds, loosely entwined in the rococo manner, around the gilt-framed white panels contained in woodwork painted grey-blue and picked out in gold leaf. One suspects Bolander was painting many of his exotics from imagination (a pineapple looks a little like a very large fircone, or an even larger loganberry) but the colour is luscious and the brushwork and composition assured. Bamboo in real life was never so pliant as it is here, providing a leisurely framework, wittily tied with wisps of string, for clusters of pompom chrysanthemums, sunflowers, a recognizable wild strawberry plant and green melons bound with striped ribbon.

The sophistication of Bolander's work at Ekolssund seems to have set new standards of technical accomplishment for Scandinavian decorative painters working in the many large houses being built, remodelled, or merely redecorated at this period. The personality of Gustav III, and his intelligent and exacting patronage, undoubtedly helped to make his fellow-Scandinavians more culturally aware, more responsive to change and less provincial. Inevitably perhaps, the tastefulness and refinement in the arts that his patronage inspired became after a time a rather anaemic correctness, which looks lifeless in comparison to the awkward but exuberant vigour of earlier baroque work. But at this stage in Swedish art, wider horizons and a new impetus were needed, which Gustav, with his deep belief in the greatness of Sweden and his wide-ranging interest in European culture, was able to provide.

At all events the Francophile 'new look' of the eighteenth century – pretty, fastidious and cosmopolitan – instantly became fashionable and inspired countless imitations throughout Scandinavia. A surprising number of these survive almost intact to this day, not only in museums (Skogaholm in the Skansen museum is an especially attractive example) but in private houses. Inevitably, as people adapted the look to different situations, adding locally made furniture with a Scandinavian feel to it, the results departed more and more from the French model, becoming simpler, less luxurious and more serious.

LEFT *The delicacy and brio of Bolander's style can be seen clearly in this corner from the painted panel shown on the opposite page.*

Yet another example of the diverse and charming styles of faux 'panel' decoration from the garret suite at Gripsholm.

Painted wall-hangings or panels, or *tapeter*, are an essential ingredient of this look, and contemporary room schemes yield countless versions ranging in style from high sophistication to artless rusticity. Wall-hangings, or *bonad*, descend from the woven hangings used as early as the twelfth century in Scandinavia. In baroque decoration they often hung loose over walls that were still simply boarded over in vertical planks on top of an original shell of logs. Some fairly grand houses were constructed of timber and stretched canvas *tapeter* masked the underlying construction perfectly, giving a smooth, elegant, unified appearance to a room. (Stretched canvas hangings stained to resemble woven tapestries were also made in England in the sixteenth and seventeenth centuries.) Probably, too, they helped to keep rooms warmer by improving insulation; certainly woven tapestries reduced condensation in stone-walled interiors.

The grander versions of such neo-classical rooms depended on master painters of considerable skill and experience, and records suggest that such people, whether foreign or native, were in great demand during this period. But the style was less dependent than earlier styles on carved decoration – a skill that, outside the vernacular tradition, was not highly evolved in Scandinavia – and the essential decorative elements were quite simple. A *trompe-l'oeil* moulding, or a simple border of husks or pearls, with a modest floral swag centred above, were all that was needed to fill a panel. Combining several pastel colours, one for the 'panels', one for the surrounds, one for the decorative work, was a further refinement within the scope of an ordinary painter. The ingenuity with which this decorative formula was adapted to suit tiny, low-ceilinged or awkwardly shaped rooms, and the skill and taste with which colours and ornament are combined, make these eighteenth-century examples of Scandinavian decorative work a rich field for study today. Some of the most attractive examples of all come from the garrets occupied by gentlemen- and ladies-in-waiting at Gripsholm, and the Haga Pavilion, where a simplified treatment using pale colours and meticulously painted 'frames' of ornament, has exceptional charm. This type of decoration can be used effectively in modern rooms, which tend to lack definition, to give them a structured, finished look; and, of course, it is perfectly suited to eighteenth-century rooms anywhere, however small.

The illusionist painting and decorative paint effects that made such a splash of colour in baroque interiors are much less in evidence in the eighteenth century. Marbling of a refined sort was used for the tops of commodes and pier tables, in addition to spattered imitations of granite and porphyry as at the Haga Pavilion. Grisaille painting over gold leaf, giving something of the effect of relief modelling in stucco, is a technique more in keeping with the fashionable look of studied elegance, and there are fine examples of this delicate but effective technique in the various Royal palaces. This small-scale grisaille work was sometimes executed on coloured backgrounds, where it anticipates the effect of Josiah Wedgwood's ornamental jasper wares. Roundels and friezes executed in this technique are often combined with 'panel' treatments with a neo-classical flavour. Another neo-classical theme, skilfully developed in the Haga Pavilion and at Marienlyst, in

A wonderful quality of light suffuses the main rooms at Beatelund reflected back from mirrors and exceptionally pretty chandeliers, hanging in groups of four in this drawing room with its remarkably preserved ceiling decoration in the baroque style painted directly onto whitewashed boards. During the Gustavian period this decoration was covered up by a false ceiling of plainly painted canvas. It was not till the grandfather of the present owner needed some wiring put in in the early years of this century that the original decoration was discovered above. To the right is a glimpse through into the 'verdure' painted hall shown on page 96, on the left a dining room in grey and white. Carpets and furniture have been collected over the years, and are of high quality.

ABOVE *Stoves of this elongated shape, perched on feet (brass here but more often wood, despite the risk of fire) are among the earliest to be found in Scandinavia, Sweden especially. This early eighteenth-century example is in blue-and-white tiles decorated in Chinoiserie style, though probably made in Europe.*

ABOVE *Another early stove, with wooden feet this time, from Skogaholm at Skansen. This stove, with its large awkwardly placed flue, has all the air of a later interpolation in a baroque room scheme. Rich green glazes like this were usually considered rustic, and reserved for country houses.*

ABOVE *Neat and even dainty, this columnar stove shows the start of the neo-classical influence that was to turn all* kakelungen *into shining white pillars. Gustav III chose one of these – in the most austere style – for his Haga dining room.*

ABOVE *Gleaming white faience and polished brass for a stove that stands out handsomely against the hardwood panelling and painted ruins that give an Anglophile air to this attractively cosy drawing room at Skansen.*

ABOVE *A primitive-looking, but charming, small stove from Gripsholm, with an enormous steel door that opens wide to allow more radiant heat into the room. Though the stove here is smaller than usual, the firebox is larger, so the result was probably the same amount of warmth in the room.*

ABOVE *Scandinavian-style marbling on the diagonal makes a pretty decoration for a small blue-and-white stove with wooden feet. Assembling the tiles so that the diagonals carried on round must have been quite a complex business. Antique stoves are eagerly sought today.*

ABOVE *A handsome neo-classical style stove from the marbled dining-room at Sturehov. This stove has an exceptionally large firebox, reaching down to the floor, and must have given off immense heat since, it is also exceptionally tall.*

ABOVE *A neo-classical stove, in ivory and green, in a wonderful pea-green interior with painted borders and bobbled frieze from Skansen. All the furnishings to this little house are original. The curtain treatments are especially interesting.*

Denmark, was decoration in the Pompeiian style, with 'grotesques' painted in the style and colours of the Roman wall paintings found in the recently excavated Pompeii.

At this time decorative painting makes an unexpected appearance, for Scandinavia, on floors. (Painted floors were also to be found in English houses in the eighteenth and early nineteenth centuries.) There was a vogue for painting floors in large chequers, or lattice patterns, directly on to the floorboards, in imitation of marble paving and parquet de Versailles. While it seems a pity to cover the wonderful blanched boards of the traditional Scandinavian floor, one can see that these simple visual deceptions gave formal rooms (they are often used in ballrooms) a more finished appearance. Usually the simpler the design, the more attractive it looks; plain grey-and-black squares, for instance, in matt distemper, looking more elegant than the shinily varnished and busily marbled squares at Fosseholm, near Oslo.

One surprising survival, given its great age, is the painted floor cloth at Tullgarn (another royal residence outside Stockholm), which must be one of the very few left in existence. Floor cloths of painted and varnished canvas enjoyed a vogue all over Europe in the late eighteenth century, being cheap, practical and decorative. The Tullgarn floor cloth was made to fit an irregularly shaped room and such customized floor cloths were quite common. The predominant colours, which pick up other colours in the room, are pale blue and off-white and the design consists of compartments containing floral motifs, in a style rather reminiscent of Savonnerie carpets. The surface is a little worn and threadbare here and there, but considering how many feet must have walked across it, the original paint has survived remarkably well.

Although stoves had been in use in Scandinavia since medieval times, the really great innovation in domestic comfort at this period was the introduction of the *kakelungen*, the huge faience (glazed ceramic tile) stoves where quite a small fire in the lower compartment heats a complicated system of ducts and heat-storage bricks. Most of these stoves were produced by the Marieberg factory between 1758 and 1788 and there are some good examples to be seen in Sturehov Manor, near Stockholm.

Kakelungen were extremely effective heat-providers and much less messy than open fires. They could also, as the ones at Sturehov prove, be superbly handsome and colourful objects within a room, but positioning them obviously caused some difficulties. It was acceptable to plumb the stove into the existing fireplace in the case of a central hearth, but when the existing fireplace was – as were many earlier ones – built across one corner of the room, this upset the Scandinavian passion for symmetry. Painted *trompe-l'oeil* once again came to the rescue; in the opposite corner to the stove a cupboard was built which was externally its twin, and this was then painted to match the glazed tiles of the real stove. At Ekolssund the painter had fun with the detail, his brass fire door, knobs and handles are so convincing one really has to feel to be sure that they are only painted wood.

While the simpler types of painted illusionism – graining, marbling, bold grisaille – lost their appeal at this time, there was a limited demand in the most sophisticated aristocratic circles for *trompe-l'oeil* of the

Which of the stoves is a cupboard? Quite frequently, where stoves installed at a later date into an existing corner chimney were thought to unbalance a room, a clever carpenter was called in to build a wooden replica to stand opposite, so that not only was symmetry restored, but useful storage space was also provided. The entrance hall to Svindersvik near Stockholm has a similar pair. The trompe-l'oeil *on the painted stove at Ekolssund (the one on the right) is especially skilful.*

highest order: the sort of elaborate visual entertainment that has always had its aficionados. The most famous example, at Åkerö, was commissioned from the court painter Johan Pasch by Carl Gustav Tessin, former ambassador to Versailles, and its fame must have spread, because imitations began to appear in other fashionable interiors. Perhaps the most attractive is the fascinating room at Olsboda, in Narke, where walls painted a deep apricot are hung with an apparently random assortment of everyday things – a broad-brimmed hat, iron keys on a ring, a satchel, boot brushes, a pipe rack and a Delft tobacco jar. The charm of the Olsboda room, apart from the wonderful colours and deft precision of the painting, is its way of ushering visitors into the apparently living presence of its long-dead owner; these mundane objects, imbued with the personality of their owner, paint a character sketch more vivid than many actual portraits; one has the sense that he has just left the room and will be back in a moment.

WOOD FINISHES

Graining, that is the imitation in paints and glazes of characteristic wood grain and figuring, usually of the more precious hardwoods, has traditionally ranked alongside marbling as the supreme expression of decorative painterly skill. While the end results may look very different, the essential sleight of hand involved is much the same, and in fact marbling and graining were usually practised together. An exceptionally gifted marbler and grainer, like Thomas Kershaw, whose painted boards took all the prizes at a Paris Exhibition, is in effect a walking timberyard and marble quarry, his head packed with natural formations plus the painterly processes most apt for reproducing them to order. As with all skilled trades, marbling and graining has its mystique and its trade secrets, dodges and discoveries that give a finer surface or more transparent colour, or create complex effects simply. One grainer uses flat beer for overglazing, another polishes his surfaces with French chalk or rotten-stone, or makes use of a crumpled chamois leather (today, plastic bag) to create certain effects. In the final analysis, however, skill in these techniques is born of observation, practice and taste.

The popularity of graining has tended to follow, historically, the fashion for decorative hardwood, both as in furniture and joinery. The first sizeable wave of grained effects seems to have been a response to the seventeenth-century European fashion for exotic and dramatically figured woods, like oyster walnut, or elaborate marquetry surfaces in the Dutch manner. The graining of this period (excellent examples can be seen at Belton, and at Ham House, both in England) tends to be strong, with bold markings and dark colours, an effect that stands out across a room. It is more like a caricature than a facsimile of the real thing.

Some of the bold, early graining has the look of having been done with water-based (or watery, as in beer, vinegar etc) glazes rather than oil-based types. Transparency, plus a degree of sticking power, was what grainers looked for as a glazing medium, and at different times, a wide range of media has been tried in search of the ideal substance: beer, vinegar, honey, blood, egg white, and, latterly, Coca Cola. The second wave of graining, during the nineteenth century, coincided with the great popularity of furniture in mahogany, and in exotically grained wood such as burr maple, sycamore and satinwood. By

this period, graining techniques were becoming more refined, and skilled nineteenth-century grainers could replicate precious woods so closely that one has to inspect their work carefully to tell the difference. Painstaking naturalism characterizes most nineteenth-century graining, and this has been the most influential style of graining up till the present day, which is seeing a further revival of this craft as a disguise for modern joinery materials such as medium density fibreboard. The paler-coloured wood effects are the most popular today, with old pine graining in demand for boardrooms, bars and hotel foyers – a development which would surely have raised a smile among the Scandinavian grainers of old who spent so much time graining pine to look like Cuban mahogany.

Graining as a decorative disguise did not achieve really widespread popularity in Scandinavia until the nineteenth century. Earlier the usual method of disguising wood was to paint it. Scandinavia produced, and still does produce, many highly skilled grainers of the naturalistic sort, but expert as this work is it differs hardly at all from similar work being done elsewhere. To an outsider looking for decorative effects with a distinctively Scandinavian feel, by far the most interesting development in the craft was in the rustic or provincial work which mostly dates from the first part of the nineteenth century. In style it is a throwback to the earlier, seventeenth-century style of graining, forceful, with strong contrasts that jump out across a room. But the Scandinavian provincial painters took the process further, as they always tended to do, inventing bold and bizarre effects which are far removed from sedate mahogany, and constitute a rumbustious folk tradition in their own right. Working with enormously facile and manipulable glazes of various sorts, usually in black over a dull red, they used everything and anything

The simplest form of wood graining was merely to paint a piece in English red, and overglaze it to give the softened red-brown shown on this distinguished eighteenth-century bureau, with its dramatic black-and-white decoration. The colour is no more than a gesture towards mahogany, but at this period and on this type of superior traditional provincial furniture, that was as far as graining needed to go.

that came to hand, starting with their hands (fingertips, or the side of the palm), and progressing through adventitious tools such as scraps of card, scrumpled cloth, corks and so forth, to sketch in rapidly a wild but pleasingly important painted effect over a simple chest of drawers, or a pull-out bed. Anyone who has experimented with effects of this kind knows that the secret is to call a halt before things get out of hand. Innate good sense, probably backed up by cost-effective considerations, seems to have guided these country grainers towards a well-judged eccentricity which stops short this side of anarchy. The appeal of grained work of this period, more of it observable in Denmark than elsewhere in Scandinavia, is the transformation which a few heroic scribbles can wreak on the most ordinary deal chest. Inexplicably, given their entrancing variety and decorativeness, the appeal of these examples of rustic graining seems to have been overlooked by people today searching for fast, striking paint effects with a country feel.

Unlike the older tradition of painted furniture, where the underlying wood shows through thin, translucent coats of linseed-oil paint, the surfaces to be grained were first covered with an obliterating paint, dull red where mahogany was the effect intended, sometimes ochre yellow, as a base for oak or walnut graining, though in each case the resemblance to the wood in question was often purely notional. What customers wanted, it seems, was lots of strong pattern. One finds chest fronts tightly packed with oyster shapes, presumably a distant folk memory of earlier marquetry, and whole surfaces laboriously doodled in a vermicular pattern, closer to contemporary textile patterns than wood. There is much bold play with the mirror-image effects found in furniture made from – or veneered with – mahogany heartwood, surfaces striped like Douanier Rousseau tigers, or spotted and blotched like bizarre orchids. In rustic pieces, there seems to have been little attempt to work up a convincing gloss finish; French polishing was reserved for the imposing pieces destined for bourgeois homes, such as bureaux, roll top desks, and the sofas enclosed between cabinets referred to elsewhere.

Wild graining effects

Our example can only suggest the variety of graining effects to be found in Scandinavia, but they are chiefly intended to show how easily some of the rustic finishes can be imitated.

Rustic mahogany

On a base coloured, and covered, with an opaque paint tinted with venetian red (again red oxide primer can serve, doctored a little to enrich the colour), a thin dark overglaze, tinted with either black or Vandyke brown (which is softer), was brushed on, one surface at a time. Before the glaze had begun to dry off, loose swirls were brushed in using a little more of the glaze colour on the brush. There is no serious attempt to imitate natural grain, or the way grain would fall in the hands of a cabinetmaker. The looping shapes are more about the pleasure of making bold shapes quickly and fluently. These markings are on a large scale, which is characteristic. One series of loops like those shown here may easily suffice to grain one side of a chest of drawers; two or three in diagonal parallel lines will fill in the whole front surface. Sometimes, as a refinement, the edges of drawer fronts may be grained differently, a painted line indicating banding, and short brush strokes fringing the outer edges in a crude imitation of an effect popular on the better veneered furniture of the late eighteenth and early nineteenth centuries. Usually the top of a grained chest, or cupboard, was grained to match, but occasionally it was marbled, in equally impressionistic style, or given a faux porphyry or granite finish. It would be sensible today to give a piece grained in this style one or two coats of clear varnish, to seal and protect it.

A transparent black overglaze is brushed over the dull red base colour used for mahogany graining.

RIGHT *Using a standard-sized paintbrush, large loops are brushed over the wet glaze, to create the effect shown here, imitating mahogany heartwood in a bold, primitive way.*

RIGHT *Rustic graining goes for drama and symmetry, as in the parallel loops shown, rather than realism based on close observation of actual wood-grain patterns.*

Rustic freestyle

The cult of expertise today has given many people a false impression that paint effects require a panoply of specialist tools and equipment, and that these will somehow, magically, produce the required effect. The truth is, annoyingly, that in practised hands the most basic, ad hoc materials, like those shown here, produce excellent results. An hour's experiment with a piece of notched card or plastic will teach you more about the possibilities of this branch of finishing, than a box full of draggers, floggers, softeners and sword liners. Improvisation is very much in the spirit of the original work, where anything handy with decorative potential must have been tried and played with experimentally.

For the example shown here a surface painted in a pale buff shade was overglazed with a burnt umber/black colour, made from the usual half-and-half mixture of linseed oil and turpentine, but with artist's oils rather than dry colour as the tinting agent.

While this was still wet and malleable, various effects were created. The simplest, often seen on peasant furniture, uses the side of one's fist to stamp repeating, just overlapping, shapes over the whole surface. This was almost certainly the method used to create the oyster shapes already mentioned.

Another favourite effect with Scandinavian grainers involves the interplay of bold decorative shapes with a closely patterned background. The background patterning here was created, very fast but effectively, with a scrumpled plastic bag lightly pounced over the entire wet glazed surface. This creates a busy decorative texture not unlike the effect obtained by the vermicular doodling mentioned above, but in reverse, the doodling appearing pale on a dark ground.

With a small, soft, bendy piece of rubber or plastic or card, curious 'carrot' shapes are produced by scraping off the glaze in a controlled stroke which executes a sort of quarter turn halfway and is allowed to taper off to a point. Used in various ways, like sun rays, or more abstractly, these odd but elegant shapes appear frequently on old grained items. They work best where the background surface has been distressed as shown, so modifying the contrast between the dark glaze and pale base colour.

For a different, but equally bold, result, our last example shows the same wet glaze being 'combed' with a piece of notched card or plastic, to make striking scallopped patterns, joining up roughly in figures of eight. With a little practice techniques like these are exceptionally useful as starting points for a decorative scheme, because they all give the most impact possible in the least time.

A buff base colour is overglazed with a deep brown black glaze made with linseed oil and turps tinted with artists' oils, for flow, rather than dry colour. This is the malleable base for graining effects of a rustic kind. Glazes made with vinegar or beer were often used in much the same way.

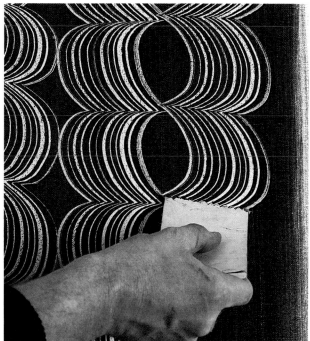

ABOVE *Why buy more equipment, was how the rural painters reasoned, when the side of a balled fist makes an effective stamp on a wet glaze. This sausage effect is seen everywhere.*

ABOVE *Combing with notched card creates the sort of juicy stripes and curves which figure in so many rustic grained effects. The ground colour was often ochre, or red, rather than white.*

BELOW *Bunched-up-kitchen wipes pressed into the glaze create the sort of crinkly pattern, using adventitious means, which appealed so strongly to these country craftsmen.*

BELOW *Another piece of card is being used to 'wipe out' curious carrot shapes, which quite often appear on old pieces, often lined up like vertebrae in imitation of heart-wood, or bunched in corners, for purely decorative effect.*

Faux Biedermeyer graining

The Biedermeyer fashion for pale blonde woods, discreetly grained, led to a new repertoire of graining effects of the sort shown in our last example. Faux panels, executed with brushwork in wet glaze to suggest pale wood, and then sharpened with dark painted lines added with a sword liner or sable pencil, sketch in a convincing impression of the type of woodwork and furnishing which was admired throughout Europe during the 1830s, and later.

After pencilling in the panel outlines on the off-white paint ground, a tawny overglaze, tinted with raw sienna, ochre and a little burnt umber, was brushed in broadly to create the darker blonde framework. The brushwork was distressed lightly, with the bristle tips applied in a slightly wavering line, then cross-hatched as shown to create a richer texture. The fine wavering lines on the fielded panels were touched in with a fine sable brush. A stronger brushful of the same glaze implied a darker wood on the mouldings, and when dry this was emphasized by lining in burnt umber with a sword liner, to create shadows and sharp edges, also the fine joins where one section of wood butts onto another. When dry the whole surface was lightly overglazed once more with a barely tinted glaze, yellowish with ochre. As a final touch the whole surface was varnished with a clear, satin-finish varnish.

OPPOSITE *Blond woods such as fruitwood, sycamore and maple became immensely fashionable during the first part of the nineteenth century, and coalesce in the decorative style known as Biedermeyer. Here, Biedermeyer-type panelling is painted in trompe-l'oeil on a flat white ground to show the scope of this technique. The tawny 'frame' of wet glaze has been* distressed lightly with bristle tips in two directions to give the streaky grain shown, while the slim darker moulding is added with a darker brown, lined out finely in black. Faint grain lines in black are touched in on the field of the panels with a fine sable brush.

ABOVE *This detail shows how the panel effect shown opposite can be stacked up with additional devices suggestive of jambs and architraves to give the impression of twin doors of blond satinwood with ebony banding in the Biedermeyer style. This is a highly decorative use of graining quite often seen on furniture and also in dignified commercial interiors such as boardrooms and foyers.*

PAINTED FURNITURE

In medieval Europe, painted furniture was the norm. The fact that painted furniture survived in Scandinavia into the last century is yet another feature of the strong vernacular or folk tradition of the region. Scandinavian painted furniture was chiefly made from native softwoods such as spruce and pine, but also from birch, which is technically a hardwood. Massive oak chests (showing traces of colour) from the early medieval period in Scandinavia recall a time when oak – always prized for shipbuilding – was more common. Medieval and renaissance furniture, usually sturdy and simple, features shallow curved ornament on all surfaces – strapwork on grander pieces, simple geometric patterns and roundels on peasant furniture – and was painted in several colours, red, yellow and green being especially popular. From the seventeenth century on, Scandinavian furniture can be broadly divided into two types – a robust peasant style featuring carved relief, painted in bright colours, and more cosmopolitan, elegant painted pieces for the middle and upper classes. Most of this type was made by city craftsmen; country furniture was made by provincial tradesmen, some of whom only turned to carpentry in winter to supplement seasonal work as fishermen, farmers and so on.

Country cousin to a serpentine-fronted commode, finished in a translucent garnet red, this robustly handsome piece from Beatelund epitomizes a sophisticated/provincial style of Scandinavian furniture much admired today. Though unpretentious, it is a pedigree piece, well made and finely and unhurriedly painted to exacting traditional standards.

ABOVE *This detail of the painted rococo desk shown below highlights the Scandinavian painter's skill in texturing a simple paint finish, via many coats of thin colour lightly abraded till it seems integral with the piece itself. Finely finished water gilding, as here, is a typical embellishment on superior furniture.*

But a great deal of the most attractive painted furniture falls somewhere between these two extremes of urban elegance and rustic solidity. This type is probably best defined as 'provincial', but is in a more restrained style and finish than the highly decorated peasant pieces; it might have been made by the same provincial workshop as the latter, to commission, or it might have been the work of estate carpenters producing furniture for their *slott* or *herrgård* to a brief laid down by the noble or his steward. At all events it tended towards a sophisticated simplicity, the heavier but still shapely counterpart in painted pine of a bombé commode, for instance, or one of the charming writing-tables with a nest of drawers at one end, so they could be stood at right angles to the wall, which are such characteristically Scandinavian eighteenth-century pieces. The paint finish, typically, is in one colour, smoky blue-green or deep red, applied in many transparent layers for a japanned effect, relieved perhaps by a sparing touch of gold leaf. Such pieces have a classic look that is at home in any context, and makes them eagerly collected today.

Scandinavian painted furniture is invariably of high quality, with regard to both the joinery and the actual paint application. In the rest of Europe, where 'serious' furniture was made from hardwood by *ébénistes* and cabinet-makers, painted furniture tended to be pretty but flimsy, gesso and paint used to disguise poor-quality softwood and less-than-perfect construction. Scandinavian furniture makers, however, worked with the finest well-seasoned, straight-grained pine; they were skilled and conscientious furniture makers; and they were part of a long tradition of painting and decorating wooden surfaces of every kind. All this, together with two qualities that seem innately Scandinavian, a feeling for form and balance, and a sensitive instinct for colour, combine to make their painted furniture exceptional, a fact which has belatedly been recognized by the Swedish government, which in 1989 banned the export of furniture over a century old.

RIGHT *Desks, or writing tables, of this type, designed to stand at right angles to a wall to make the most of natural light from French-style windows, are an outstandingly graceful feature of many eighteenth-century Scandinavian interiors. The one shown here, partnered by a gilt 'klysmos' chair almost identical to the ones Masreliez designed for the Haga pavilion, is an especially fetching rendering of a subtle blue-green-grey paint colour which has come to seem characteristically Swedish.*

This fastidious, pretty grouping of painted furniture and porcelain in one of the sensitively restored interiors at Aelfsunda, a miniature slott *not far from Stockholm, is* interesting for the insight it gives into intelligent contemporary handling of traditional Scandinavian themes. Marbling in subdued colours, 'panel' effects in minimal trompe-l'oeil combine with off-white paintwork rubbed back to the wood, and a simple boarded ceiling, to create a composed, well-mannered effect.

The lack of natural clay deposits in rocky Sweden made decorated ceramics, such as the plates displayed in this corner of an old farm kitchen/living room, into valued status symbols. Here the local painter has given the plates deliberate prominence with a rich, dusky colour scheme of warm red-brown, lightened by bands of floral motifs in vivid green/blue. Note especially the lively texture of the paintwork, rich as old polished leather, a little scuffed and darkened with handling.

Pieces painted for the peasant market (or by the peasants themselves) tend to be colourful and striking. This can be as restrained as a little carved decoration picked out in red on a blue-grey background, though the full blaze of polychrome decoration on a piece from Dalarna, or one decorated in the *rosmålning* style of western Norway is more characteristic. Different regions, or rather the painters of different regions, tended to evolve distinctive painting styles, so that an expert can tell whether a cupboard comes from Skåne or Hålsingland, Fyn or Jutland, Telemark or Bergen, whereas the uninitiated eye registers uninhibited colour and generous scale, at first glance, and a liking for crowded surfaces (*horror vacui* is very pronounced in peasant decoration) and carefully poised symmetry of shapes, like Rorschach blots, in full colour, at the second. Symmetry was a proof of skill as well as formally satisfying to the peasant eye, because (as *rosmaling* teachers are fond of explaining) it is far from simple to repeat on the left hand side of the design the shapes and flourishes that flowed so easily on the right. The elaborate decoration that appears on much of this type of painted furniture includes effects such as graining, marbling, dotting (with finger tip and paint), flicking in little 'whiskers', all of which give twice the drama for half the work. Figurative devices such as bouquets or roses were roughed out using templates and stencils. Rather than outlining in pencil, it seems likely a sharp knife was drawn round a template, just deep enough to score the wood, as in a strong light the scored lines delineating motifs can still be seen on some decorated pieces.

ABOVE *The intense blues of so much old Scandinavian painted furniture have a lyrical quality which often comes across most poignantly where the painted pieces are bone simple, as here. The old paint surfaces have worn bare on all leading edges and working tops, such as the desk flap in our photograph.*

RIGHT *This painted secretaire or bureau dated 1796 has been given the decorative treatment reserved for an important peasant, or provincial, item of furniture – floral panels and a painted inscription, dusky graining for background texture, sprightly touches of* trompe-l'oeil *to suggest a carved cornice and vivid picking out on the drawer fronts. As the painted swags on the plank wall indicate, this was a household which enjoyed and commissioned painted objects.*

ABOVE *Primitive grained effects were just becoming popular in the early nineteenth century when this small desk was made and decorated, and the patterns shown here are halfway between the 'farmer marbling' effects so fashionable heretofore, and the bold and bizarre rustic graining finishes – combed, stamped, ragged and otherwise distressed, supposedly in imitation of expensive hardwoods – which were to flood the market later in the century.*

The paints used by Scandinavian furniture-makers were dry pigments bound with egg yolk, as in egg tempera, or with buttermilk, as in casein paint, or with animal or fish glue, as in distemper or the clear wash of colour known in eighteenth-century England as 'clair collé'. None of these binding materials is ideal (egg tempera, for instance, hardens in time to a toughness as of enamel, but takes weeks to dry out thoroughly), but when the use of linseed oil as binder and medium for pigments finally became established in Scandinavia, it became the most popular medium for furniture painting. Its drying time could be hastened if turpentine was added to the mixture, and carefully applied, in the many thin coats prescribed by all old painting manuals, it produced a fine, smooth and durable finish. But the great feature of oil-based paint was the glowing translucency it gave colours and, in addition, the viscous richness of tone that brought dark colours to life.

Oil-based colour could be applied directly to the sized or undercoated wood, or laid over a foundation of gesso, to give colours increased luminosity by providing a smooth, reflective undercoat. Whether or not gesso was used, the wood needed to be fine grained and free from blemishes. Putty was the only filler allowed, and it was used very sparingly. Surfaces were smoothed with cuttlefish bone before paint was applied. In most cases the painted decoration even on a much-used piece has lasted well and is still clear and vivid, if a little worn around the handles and leading edges. As linseed oil paint ages, its transparency increases, and the grain and texture of the wood beneath actively contribute to the surface interest, giving an effect at once livelier and gentler than anything opaque colour could achieve.

Though strong colours are the norm, it is rare that one sees a garish piece. Many colour schemes that sound unpromising work splendidly in reality; some of the most effective schemes combine small doses of brilliant colour with quite large areas of drab colour and some black. The colours that are most often associated with peasant decoration, however, are the cool or thundery blues based on cobalt tempered with raw umber, garnet red of the type known as English Red, and a soft, dim mid-green, all of which make good background to splashes of bright colour.

Peasant furniture was primarily functional, and if it could serve two or more functions simultaneously, so much the better. An early example is the turn-over bench, descended from a medieval European design, which stood alongside the dining table in some *stuga* interiors, with a wall-hung bench on the far side. The backs of these benches pivoted, so that by simply turning the back over from one side of the bench to the other, the seat could face the table or face back into the room. Then there were combined bench-chests and other hybrid pieces: chests of drawers topped by dresser-type shelves and a bureau with pigeonholes, drawers, and even a roll top grafted on to a

OPPOSITE *This marbled secretaire/cupboard from the northern Swedish province of Hålsingland is decorated with typical vigour and confidence. The* characteristic 'clouds' marbling technique of the region has been used to decorate every surface of the piece with an energy far transcending polite, urbane, upper-class prettiness.

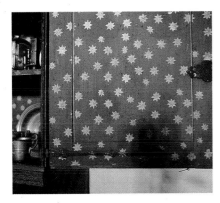

Detail from the armoire shown opposite. In close-up, the wonderfully decorative star motif used to dramatize an inky blue like a night sky, turns out to be a hand-painted device, four brushstrokes at a time, dotted about not too regularly. Stencilled stars would look too precise. Note especially the beautiful translucency of the ground colour, almost certainly a linseed oil paint coloured with Prussian blue.

cupboard bed. However, the most innovative design was surely the Gustavian bed, a vernacular reflection of the neo-classical style introduced in the reign of Gustav III. This, with its close relation, the *dragsoffan*, might well be the prototype of our modern sofa-bed. Folded up for the day with the bedding stored inside, the Gustavian bed looks like a cross between a long narrow sofa and a bateau bed, the back usually prettily carved and decorated. At night the front of the piece pulled out to bed length. The *dragsoffan* differed chiefly in having a lid showing that it was also intended as a seat. Gustavian beds have a slightly formal air, more suggestive of the salon than the *stuga*, and it is perhaps a surprise to discover just how many of them were bought by peasant households. Probably, like the splendid Mora long-case clocks, which came in both grandfather and grandmother styles, the Gustavian bed was a status symbol. But, as an impromptu double bed for guests, it was also useful and, with its carved and painted back, sometimes echoed by garlands on the front panels, it could be very decorative.

The masterpiece of rustic painted furniture is surely the traditional clock known as 'the Bride of Ångermanland'. Ångermanland is one of the most northerly Swedish provinces, where people lived by fishing and trapping. Seizing on the obviously female curves of the conventional rococo clockcase, round moon face set above an hour-glass figure, an inspired eighteenth-century furniture maker added carved details reproducing the wedding regalia of local brides – diadem, wedding crown, necklace, bridal belt and hanging purse. The carved ornament was then painted in vivid bridal colours, and the whole effect must have been as irresistible to contemporaries as it is to us today, because such clocks became famous and popular throughout Sweden.

RIGHT *A row of tiny carved crosses along the back gives a slightly funereal aspect to an otherwise modest, prettily painted Gustavian bed of the simpler sort. By pulling the front forward, the bed could be extended to sleep two people in tolerable comfort. During the day the rolled-up bedding, stored in the base, made a reasonably comfortable seat.*

Cupboards, or armoires, specially designed to show off prized household possessions ranging from stacks of folded linen sheets and tablecloths to burnished pewter, or even family silver, are found all over Scandinavia, mostly dating from the eighteenth and nineteenth centuries. The Norwegians call them Fatehbur. *This unusually striking* example, with its simple but highly original star decoration on a huge ground over all the interior surfaces, is now in Gripsholm, one of the Royal castles of Sweden, but must have originated somewhere lower down the social scale. Here it is being used to set off a fine collection of old pewter. When the Fatehbur *is closed up, nothing on the outside suggests* the exciting display within. Doors on such cupboards are hinged to be opened out flat, as shown.

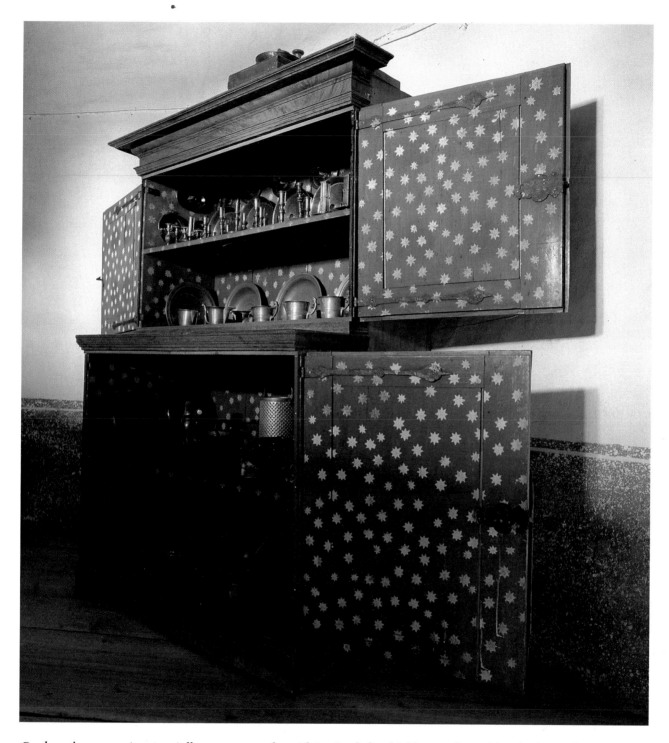

Cupboards, or armoires, specially designed to show off prized household possessions ranging from stacks of folded linen sheets and tablecloths to burnished pewter, or even family silver, are found all over Scandinavia, mostly dating from the eighteenth and nineteenth centuries. The Norwegians call them Fatehbur. *This unusually striking* example, *with its simple but highly original star decoration on a huge ground over all the interior surfaces, is now in Gripsholm, one of the Royal castles of Sweden, but must have originated somewhere lower down the social scale. Here it is being used to set off a fine collection of old pewter. When the* Fatehbur *is closed up, nothing on the outside suggests* the exciting display within. Doors on such cupboards are hinged to be opened out flat, as shown.

Following France, pale colours sparked by gilding came into fashion in Scandinavia in the latter part of the eighteenth century. Existing paintwork in the darker colours of the baroque was either painted over, as in the seventeenth-century panelled room at Skogaholm pictured here, or covered up with stretched canvas *tapeter*. Unusually, the decorated baroque ceiling in the hallway at Skogaholm has been left intact. Chairs painted en suite *with the decor are another late eighteenth-century feature; straight-legged chairs like these are in Gustavian style. Panelling and furniture alike would have been painted in lead white, which turns a silvery grey colour with age.*

Delicate rococo wall painting, in the faux 'panel' style at Skogaholm is echoed in the charming carved top-knot on the painted chair back, which has been picked out in pastel shades of grey, yellow and green.

At the other end of the social scale, painted furniture, after a lull during the baroque period when hardwood veneers and marquetry work in the Dutch manner was fashionable, swept to the forefront of fashion in the second half of the eighteenth century. Taking their cue from the French *ébénistes*, and in some cases from English cabinet-makers like Hepplewhite, Swedish craftsmen began to produce furniture in a much lighter style, ornamented with carved flowers, bows and husks. Though these pieces resembled furniture being made elsewhere in Europe, what gives them a distinctively Scandinavian look is a certain primness about the overall shape (straight legs were preferred to curved ones, for instance) and the prevalence of paint finishes in pastel shades and matt, chalky textures. In some instances a little gilding was added, for sparkle and richness, but perhaps the most attractive examples are the ones on which the only decoration is in the carved ornament, usually picked out in contrasting pale shades. Characteristic pieces in this style are elegant little chairs with carved back splats, long narrow sofas, sometimes caned for lightness, narrow beds with carved ends designed to be pushed sideways to the wall with a draped canopy suspended above, a profusion of mirrors in all shapes and sizes, and carved and painted, or gilt, candle holders and sconces of enchanting prettiness. A typical mirror, oval or rectangular and often with detachable candle holders, has a simple, lightly carved frame painted pale grey, or light blue, with a prettily carved topknot of roses and lovers' knots which may be coloured pink and green. This rococo style was followed by Gustavian neo-classicism, with its preference for symmetry and straight lines. Carved ornament is more restrained, and colours are cooler – straw yellow, pearl grey, muted blue. The pieces were usually gessoed before painting, to give a very smooth and refined surface.

The understated elegance of Gustavian painted furniture immediately made it the favourite style of furnishing for the more prosperous Scandinavian homes, and today it is rare to find a home that does not have at the very least some painted *Gustaviansk* chairs, often set round a painted table *en suite*. Modern reproductions are also available, and are among the most successful 'repro' pieces on the market, although the eye wearies of the monotony of the matt-grey paint in the factory finish that lacks the delicate final glazes of old pieces. Professional decorative painters in Sweden are often asked to 'antique' these mass-produced Gustavian style pieces, adding thin glazes to soften the blank opaque paint finish, and sometimes a little painted decoration, painted lines, or a few flowers. It is interesting to note that Carl Larsson's house, as shown in *Ett Hem*, contains various Gustavian pieces, white-painted sofa and chairs, mixed in with provincial or peasant pieces, striped floor rugs, white muslin drapes, and the hand-painted or stencilled touches that the Larssons added themselves. Any interior decorator wishing to create a distinctively Scandinavian look today tends to abstract much the same elements as did Larsson: although these were not necessarily contemporaneous, they demonstrably look well together, and evoke a serene but unpretentious elegance which is easy to live with. Even so, an outsider might cavil that it is almost too cool and orderly, and long to inject – as indeed Larsson did, with his painter's eye – unexpected colour and more textures.

Many Gustavian painted pieces were complemented by the use of brightly checked cotton or linen fabrics for chair seats and bed hangings. Checked dust covers were fairly standard through eighteenth-century Europe, and were often left in place to protect more valuable silk or needlework beneath, but it remained a Scandinavian discovery to make use of gay and simple checked fabric for its own sake. Nowadays, a pair of painted chairs with checked seat cushions, in red and white or blue and white, standing either side of an alcove bed draped with the same checks, creates an image that is both quintessentially Scandinavian and contemporary in its unpompous simplicity.

Painted pieces in the peasant style continued to be made until the late nineteenth century, but painted furniture fell out of favour several decades earlier as the market for middle-class furniture expanded. This was the era of upholstered comfort, and the prosperous air of polished dark wood. In Denmark, especially, many large veneered pieces of furniture were produced, including tall bureau desks with bombé doors to their little cupboards and astonishing sofas like catafalques, with seating enclosed between veneered cupboards – useful perhaps, but of elephantine ugliness. In the wake of these changes in taste, the only innovation in paint effects was the development of graining, which imitated, with widely differing degrees of skill, admired woods like mahogany, satinwood, and maple. The best Scandinavian graining was very skilled, and remains so to this day, even when painters use Coca Cola instead of flat beer for their glazes, but much modern work is insipid and to a twentieth-century eye the naïve or bizarre effects of unskilled provincial painters are often more attractive. The inventiveness and freedom of their effects, which include tigerish stripes produced by combing, stippling with an almost furry appearance, vermicular patterning in black on red or tawny brown, rustic chests grained with bold diagonal swipes, are closer to seventeenth- and eighteenth-century graining than the verisimilitude sought by most nineteenth-century grainers and marblers.

TOP LEFT AND OPPOSITE *The classic image of the rococo Scandinavian interior: a pair of painted chairs – these are in the earlier Gustavian style, round-backed and straight-legged – covered in the same checked linen, and standing each side of a curtained bed alcove. Checked linens came in various colours – pink, red, blue, green, brown, all with white. Handwoven and of excellent quality, these coarse linens are immensely hardwearing.*

WALL PAINTING

Though Scandinavia had woven wall hangings from a very early date – the Vikings are said to have hung their walls with wool or linen coverings – there were few sixteenth-century nobles or merchants rich enough to drape their walls with costly imported tapestries of the sort to be seen at Hardwick Hall in England, in the Cluny Museum in Paris, and elsewhere in Europe. But there was a budget version of woven tapestry which had gained acceptance in Europe; this was water cloth, a painted imitation tapestry in distemper paint on canvas or hessian, of which examples survive still, as appealing in their different watery way as the more textured scenes rendered in close-woven wool tapestry. The Scandinavian painters began painting water cloths later, but on the other hand they pushed the idea further than most, and with particularly handsome effect. They became adept at rendering the bosky richness of verdure tapestries in paint, as wonderfully demonstrated at Beatelund. They were not afraid to paint out gigantic royal audience chambers, such as the one at Frederiksborg Slott in Denmark, with equally gargantuan painted canvases imitating the style, colouring, even texture, of Gobelins.

These painted imitation tapestries were, for the rich, what the spirited and colourful 'kurbits' paintings on cloth were to be for the middling poor, the first accessible form of mural decoration, on a large scale. Whole rooms, as at Beatelund, might be clothed in painted verdure scenes, sunlit glades in blue greens ochre and browns, with extraordinary effect, especially when the surrounding woodwork was painted in a toning colour, like the subtle green at Beatelund. To a modern eye these painted *tapeter* have a richly atmospheric quality as alluring as anything from Bruges or Gobelins. What they lack in warmth and texture they make up for in scene-painting intensity – really, they are like beautifully painted stage backdrops, with the extra visual mystery that these usually involve. One could almost walk into the leafy painted scenery of Beatelund; unlike a woven tapestry, it has depth, and light.

Having seen Beatelund, almost anyone with a little scene-painting or Sunday painting experience must feel an urge to try something on the same lines. So little is needed to give such a richly suggestive effect. Foliage can be blocked in rapidly with a sponge, whole scenes evoked with a few brushstrokes, and the final result, overglazed,

looks as if it had always been there. Where possible, paint such scenes on canvas, because the texture of the cloth strengthens the resemblance to tapestry. Rather than paint one hanging for a large room, paint enough hangings to entirely line a small one; this doubles and intensifies the effect. The entrance hall at Beatelund is not very large, perhaps ten or twelve feet square, but its scenic walls give it an extraordinary, fabulous beauty.

Mural effect

The mural scene shown here, as it might be one wall of a room, was painted with dazzling speed by a professional with much experience of painting mural decorations and *trompe-l'oeil*. He had visualized the scene clearly in his mind beforehand: trees, greenery, water and a suggestion of buildings in a hazy middle distance. In fact a very typical Swedish prospect. He drew the broad outlines in with his brush, with no preliminary pencil sketch. An amateur might find this alarming, though such an approach undoubtedly makes for spontaneity in the final result, an almost Chinese impressionism where a few dark blobs imply a rocky outcrop and a delicate distant spire suggests a whole village. The style is much looser, more sophisticated, than one would have found during the earlier phase of *tapeter* painting in Scandinavia, where the object was always to crowd the canvas with incident, and to work up a dense paint surface in imitation of the texture of old tapestry.

Obviously, professional skills cannot be learnt off the page, but only by practice and experiment; the skill that makes a little stand for a lot, visually, often arrives with working regularly to a deadline. However, having said this, there is much to be learnt from imaginatively following through a project like this, not least, as Roger Seamark regularly insists, that it is the final overglazing that 'makes' the thing work, softening, harmonizing, suggesting space, weather, atmosphere. Also, there is the useful lesson that in decorative art, less is usually more. A decorative essay in landscape should not be too real, detailed, fleshed out, literal. This would make it obtrusive, demanding, whereas the aim should be to create a graceful, appealing vista with plenty of space where the eye can roam and linger, but one that is low key, subordinated to the room's primary function, as a context for living. This is a refinement that too many mural painters, obsessed

with *trompe-l'oeil* surprises, overlook today, with results that are often distractingly overworked and busy or theatrical.

The wall surface in this case was first prepared with sufficient coats of white emulsion to create a blank canvas. Acrylic paints were used for the painting, but oil glazes for the finishing, because of their softness and malleable quality. A final touch of oil seems to lend a certain juiciness, too, to acrylic paint, which can look too dry, or 'lean'.

Scenes like this, borrowed from the watery vistas which abound in Scandinavia, make suitably atmospheric subjects for mural painting with water-based paint in the style of eighteenth-century panoramas. Earlier painted wall-hangings were painted in tinted distempers, which are less transparent and give a more textured surface reminiscent of woven tapestries.

The main components of the mural scene were roughed in, as already indicated, with a brush, in indeterminate colours, a fluid drawing as it were. A sponge (natural, for its irregularity) dipped in greens and greeny-browns filled in areas of foliage fast, without becoming annoyingly monotonous. Then with a fitch, foliage details such as blades of grass, rushes, branches and so on, were strengthened, still keeping to greeny-brown shades. Frequently standing back from the mural helps to suggest where more definition is needed, a stronger outline, more colour, or less. The centre of a room is about right; close-ups are not what such work is about.

Anyone who studies the example here will see that it suggests a convincing landscape with considerable economy; trees frame the foreground, a tongue of rocky land projects into a watery space in the middle distance, and the horizon is mostly closed with impressionistic shapes, and a faintly spire-like point or two. In fact much of the original blank canvas had been left that way, as lake water, and as a cloudy sky which occupies two-thirds of the space. Yet, it is there, it looks Swedish, and it is both pleasing and adequate. Left raw, unglazed, the white passages would jump out and upset the balance of the scene. This is where overglazing is so useful. The whole area was overglazed quite darkly with a burnt umber glaze rubbed on gently, round and round, with a soft rag. Areas of cloudy sky which had been suggested by a ripple of palest blue, were then wiped out, with clean rag, to create instant cloudiness, where the white base shines through. The lake water received a little of the same attention, the highlights wiped out after a moment spent gaining an overview from the other side of the room. After drying out throughly, the mural could be given a protective coat of varnish or not, depending on expected wear and tear, or indeed on how permanent you intend it to be. Varnishing 'sets' a scene, an effect that can be helpful, or not, but is optional. With egg-oil tempera, the favoured medium for fine decorative work in earlier centuries, varnishing is superfluous, since the paint itself is so tough. However, most murals, especially loose and evocative ones such as this, would need the fluency of oil paint. Varnishing here can be an improvement.

Anyone wishing to reproduce the more crowded effect of old verdure *tapeter*, of the Beatelund type, should make considerable use of spongeing, for foliage and low vegetation. The right colours are important, too, raw sienna, ochre, umber and burnt sienna work together to create the tawny areas, and these should be counterpointed by a range of blues and greeny-blues, based on Prussian blue. Ultramarine is too violet. Bear in mind that a yellowish brown overglaze will 'green' all the blues, but provide some true greens too, for contrast and richness.

Honourably battered, stained and worn down with frequent use, this battery of specialist brushes and other tools and aids is probably twice as extensive as the kit carried by itinerant rural painters a century or more ago. It is unlikely that they owned draggers, floggers and overgrainers, though goose feathers for marbling would not have presented any difficulty and most painters would have known how to make up any useful brush, such as a softener, or a fine liner, if the need arose. The stick with the padded head, or marlstick, in the centre, is an ancient device still used by sign writers for steadying the hand and brush.

ABOVE *Drawn with the brush onto a white emulsion base, this impressionistic landscape has the right looseness and airiness, though the bones of the composition are already there.*

ABOVE *A natural sponge is very useful as a rapid means of dabbing on foliage or undergrowth.*

BELOW *The completed mural awaiting its final softening overglaze.*

BELOW *The dark overglaze is swabbed on and then teased out with a soft clean cloth till the effect is satisfactory, mellow and atmospheric.*

A Gallery of Interiors

SANDEMAR

One is constantly bumping into the past, fully clothed as it were, in Scandinavia, but nowhere with a more gratifying shock of surprise than when entering Sandemar, a small seventeenth-century manor fronting the Baltic which miraculously escaped destruction by the Russian raiders who devastated Sweden's eastern seaboard in 1719. The Entrance Hall of Sandemar, with its wooden walls peopled with painted figures standing in a grisaille forest, its twin staircase with massive newel posts and balusters painted the dim grey-blue of the Baltic glimpsed at the end of an avenue of clipped yew pyramids, its little mirrored candle sconces and parchment-coloured floorboards, its rustic handling of the grand manner, is a complete seventeenth-century Swedish Baroque interior, a little hoarier than when first completed, but otherwise intact. Old structures often survive whole, but rarely in the colours and decorative clothing which their first owners chose for them, and though paint is the merest superficial skin, its survival at Sandemar brings the atmosphere, almost the taste and smell of the seventeenth century to life with extraordinary vividness.

The Entrance Hall murals and ceiling painting, in the imitation stucco or plasterwork manner of the Scandinavian baroque, appear to have been carried out in oil paint, though the surface is now so 'lean' and matt, one might suppose that distemper had been used. The blue-grey woodwork is definitely finished in oil-bound paint, now worn through to the pine beneath on the prominent edges. Blue was of course a fashionable baroque colour, but here the usual deep blue-black of interiors such as Läckö has been modified with white (possibly white lead) to give a gentler misty tone which blends suavely into the tones employed for the grisaille work on walls and ceilings. These are entirely monochrome, without the hearty splashes of red that so often accompany baroque grisaille painting in Sweden. The ceilings throughout are, as usual, of close-set boards, but painted to imitate elaborate stucco work. Even the curved fillet which acts as a cornice has been given a *trompe-l'oeil* egg-and-dart treatment along its length.

PREVIOUS PAGE *Painted fireplace at Ekolssund.*

LEFT *A head-on view of the entrance hall at Sandemar shows how imaginatively grisaille decoration has been used to create a shadowy, fantastical panorama of tones, glades and huntsmen glimpsed between* trompe-l'oeil *pilasters. Every inch of cornice and moulding has its band of grisaille decoration.*

187

ABOVE *A detail showing a trompe pilaster next to one of the fine mirrored candle sconces, their dusky paintwork just leavened with gold, which have been lighting the hall and staircase at Sandemar for almost a hundred years.*

At intervals on the walls the grisaille landscape of feathery trees springing out of a shadowy undergrowth of grasses, reeds and bracken is punctuated by *trompe-l'oeil* pilasters, fluted, with Tuscan capitals, intended to frame and distance the painted scenery, and also to provide support for the symmetrically placed painted figures whose unwinking gaze pins down the visitor at strategic points, from the corners of the hall itself, on the half-landing. Flanking the doorway to the dining room, its grey blue paint echoed in *trompe-l'oeil* pilasters either side, are two bearded huntsmen in plain jackets and breeches, wearing wide-brimmed hats and carrying muskets. These have the look of sturdy yeomen, off for a day's shooting, just as thousands of present-day Swedes and Norwegians take time off in early autumn for moose hunting. Underlining the point, a gigantic set of moose antlers hangs above the door; viewed from below these have twice the spread of deer antlers. Sets of small pointed horns decorate sloping boards either side of the hall. These hunting trophies, and the beautiful seventeenth-century sconces, their dim oval mirrors framed in dark paint and gold leaf, surmounted by carved gilt crowns, are the only superadded decoration. A pair of marble busts on the newel posts at the foot of the stairs appear to be a later inspiration, their conventional classicism oddly out of key with the remaining decoration, though their stark white silhouettes stand out impressively in the shadowy space.

RIGHT *Another detail showing one of the pair of huntsmen – identical twins – who gaze alertly at visitors entering Sandemar, muskets at the ready and game bags slung over one shoulder. The japanned long-case clock is English.*

*The staircase at Sandemar with a
classical bust on the banister.*

OPPOSITE *Double flights of stairs, with blue painted banisters of mighty girth, lead up from Sandemar's hallway to a landing furnished with comfortable chairs and sofas, now used by the family as an extra sitting room. Different sentinels, dashingly clad cavaliers with plumed hats and curls, appear halfway up, lounging gracefully against* trompe-l'oeil *pilasters. Candle sconces light the stairs, which are of great width and still carry traces of red paint, a colour which the Swedes call English, but which the English, confusingly, call Venetian red.*

The figures painted halfway up the stairs, which are broad, shallow, and of beautifully smooth pine, are of a superior social standing – gentlemen, or possibly officers, in gold-frogged scarlet uniforms, with curling plumes in their matching hats, and curly moustaches instead of beards. *Trompe-l'oeil* figures of this sort dotted about in mural paintings had appealed since at least the time of Veronese, who added shadowy figures of gardeners and other peasants in the *trompe-l'oeil* doorways of Palladian villas he decorated. Veronese took care to place his painted figures, for dramatic effect, in shadowy settings which added to the illusionism. But the painter who worked at Sandemar seems not to have been overly preoccupied with realism; the painted figures are a little below life size, and in their quaint symmetry and stiff postures more resemble that style of painted cut-out known as a Silent Companion, whose purpose remains somewhat conjectural to this day. The painted figures at Sandemar, if they embody a theme at all, must have been intended to turn people's thoughts to the pleasures of the chase; but their real purpose was surely to amuse visitors, and provide a seventeenth-century equivalent of a talking point. The similar, but less skilfully painted figures in the hallway of von Ekstedska Gården – two uniformed hussars in late seventeenth-century uniform – suggest that these painted figures were a popular baroque device for enlivening and giving scale to mural decorations.

RIGHT *Without looking contrived, or posed, the furnishings at Sandemar appear all of a piece. Here, fine old pewter, and an old horn lantern are perfectly in keeping with the smoky colouring of the place.*

Unusually, for a Scandinavian baroque interior, all the colour in Sandemar's dining room has moved from ceiling to floor, in the shape of an exceptionally beautiful Persian carpet, its smoky blues taking up the strong colouring of the paintwork, and its floral arabesques echoing the richly decorated leather tapeter. A decorated board fills in the small fireplace at either end of the room, when not in use, to cut out draughts. High-backed chairs, in polished walnut, are in period, as are the fine portraits. However one anachronism is worth noting: the glass bowl light-fitting above the chandelier. This, ingeniously, lights up both the table and chandelier itself even when the candles are not lit.

The building of Sandemar was begun towards the end of the seventeenth century by Gabriel von Falkenberg, Councillor of State and a leading noble of his day. If the grisaille decoration of the Entrance Hall suggests rusticity, a hunting lodge perhaps, the richly coloured painted tapestry (painted on canvas, in imitation of tapestry weave and shading) which covers all the walls in the great drawing room, is both more sophisticated and more palatial in style. The painted tapestry panels, in soft, warm colours beautifully set off against grey and pale blue paint on panelled doors and chimneypiece, show various scenes from the Song of Songs framed in wide borders of interlaced ornament. The illusion of tapestry is skilfully maintained by a certain dryness of technique and colouring, stippled rather than brushed, which contrasts effectively with the academic style of the portraits in oils by David Ehrenstral, Court painter to Karl XI, which are hung in the room. This technique of tapestry imitation in paint reaches its apotheosis in the immense Audience Chamber of Frederiksborg Castle in Denmark, where every inch of wallspace is painted to resemble – which it does most successfully – a colossal set of Gobelins tapestries. There, as here at Sandemar, the whole gorgeous set piece is topped by a richly decorated ceiling; Sandemar's, however, is relatively modest, stucco

imitation hung with a set of chandeliers. At Sandemar the floor also has its decoration in the shape of an immense, faded, but remarkable oriental carpet whose soft tones complement the other room surfaces. The painted tapestry colours have a wonderful glow under artificial light, and must have looked superb when the room was lit by candles and wall sconces. The colours have faded somewhat, the dominant colour today being a vivid, chalky blue, a little brighter but similar in tone to the colour used for the painted woodwork, with its grisaille panels and ornamented architraves.

Sandemar is still privately owned and much lived in. The owners have respected the historic decorations, as did their predecessors, but have not attempted to furnish the house *en suite* with none but baroque pieces. Often the resulting conflict of styles has a diluting effect on the decoration, which comes across diminished. But at Sandemar, with its fascinating counterpoint of the rustic and the sophisticated, of dignity and fantasy, the originals have such strength and character that anachronisms like standard lamps and telephones melt inoffensively into the background, and the seventeenth century stands forth unalloyed.

ABOVE *Swirly acanthus patterns on the chimney breast, and a rather more elaborate decorative treatment of the massive blue doors in the first-floor drawing-room or salon, mark a stepping up of formality as visitors process from hall and dining room to this enormous chamber, lit by no less than four chandeliers, and hung with canvases painted in imitation of woven tapestries depicting scenes from the feast of Solomon and Bathsheba. The over-door painting here shows a whippet in pursuit of a hare; dogs, horses and the hunt are a continuing preoccupation at Sandemar, which has a stud for trotting horses just inside its gates.*

RIGHT *A candle-lit detail shows more of the sumptuous colouring and border designs on Sandemar's painted wall cloths, perfectly complemented by lavish painted 'marquetry' on the oval gate-leg table. The skirting, it should be noted, is not left plain blue but decorated in smaller acanthus patterns to blend in with the overall decorative scheme.*

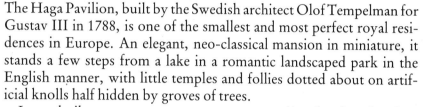

HAGA PAVILION

The Haga Pavilion, built by the Swedish architect Olof Tempelman for Gustav III in 1788, is one of the smallest and most perfect royal residences in Europe. An elegant, neo-classical mansion in miniature, it stands a few steps from a lake in a romantic landscaped park in the English manner, with little temples and follies dotted about on artificial knolls half hidden by groves of trees.

It was built as a temporary retreat, a *garçonnière*, for the King during the construction of his serious summer retreat, the Haga Palace, a monumental exercise in the neo-classical taste, a short distance away.

Too large for an ordinary *lusthus*, or pleasure pavilion, too small for a regular palace, the Haga Pavilion charms by its ambivalence. For Gustav it must have had much the same appeal as Le Petit Trianon had for that other fugitive from rigid court ceremonial, Marie-Antoinette, or that 'toy house', Strawberry Hill, had for Horace Walpole. Tedious royal duties followed the King there, of necessity, but the pretty first floor room known as the Council Chamber is furnished in the intimate, relaxed style of a smoking divan, the only concession to business a pair of writing tables for the royal secretaries which vanish into the window frames when not in use.

Seen from across the romantically beautiful park, Gustav III's Haga Pavilion is a small, neat neo-classical box with low wings either side, half hidden by immense trees. The astonishing throned Drawing Room is to the right, overlooking the lake which can just be glimpsed in the distance. In autumn, on a fine day, the air is a clear as glass in the Haga Park, now a public open space, and dogs and children race across the green levels littered with crackling yellow leaves.

ABOVE *A detail of the barracks at Haga, showing the stylishly draped and fringed entrance – all* trompe-l'oeil *– to one of the copper tents, with pretty bunched-up 'choux' each side. Blue and yellow are of course the colours of the Swedish flag.*

The great luxury for any reigning monarch, but especially one whose sexual tastes were ambiguous ('the King did not pay homage at the shrine of Venus', as one later historian delicately phrased it) and whose earlier popularity was turning sour in middle age, must always have been privacy. The Pavilion was designed to create the illusion of a fairy-tale retreat, staffed by invisible djinns. Thus the meals served in the Pavilion's imposing dining room were cooked in a kitchen banished, with all its attendant bustle and stir, to a separate building across the road, and kept warm over hotplates ingeniously built in to the vestibule. The Royal guards were housed a brisk five minutes' walk away in barracks whose utilitarian appearance was disguised under the striped painted skirts of fanciful and gigantic copper tents. The two elegant stoves, like creamware pedestals, which warmed the Mirrored Drawing Room were designed so that they could be tended and fuelled from outside the building without disturbing the King and his circle of intimates. These included talented and entertaining characters like the poet Carl Michael Bellman (the Swedish Robbie Burns), or Louis Desprez, one of the period's leading theatrical designers, as well as the predictable handsome young courtiers and aristocrats.

These meanwhile amused themselves in a setting as well appointed, fastidious, and fashionable as anything to be seen in the courts of Europe at the time. The whimsical, pretty rococo style of Gustav's youth was by now a thing of the past. The fashionable enthusiasm, which had inspired the King's extravagant collecting tour of Italy, was for the pure, severe lines and controlled use of ornament of the buildings of classical antiquity. Neo-classicism usually meant a fairly eclectic mix of the Greek and Roman architectural and decorative styles as exemplified in the classical ruins which were now required visiting on any cultured person's Grand Tour. Surviving plans and drawings show that the Haga Palace itself was to have expressed the antique spirit on a heroic scale, with colonnades and domed rotundas even more Cyclopean than those Robert Adam used in his colossal marble halls at Kedleston and Syon Park.

But the Pavilion, essentially, was a toy house, and Gustav clearly felt a more lightheartedly decorative use of neo-classical themes would be appropriate.

OPPOSITE *The Royal Guards, in Gustav's day, were quartered in the two wonderfully gaudy copper tents which stand on top of a slight rise overlooking the avenue that leads to the Pavilion itself. The tents are no more than picturesque façades. The barracks they conceal were as functional as military quarters* *anywhere, although now that one of them is a café, the internal decoration is more appealing than it ever was in the eighteenth century. 'Tent' follies turn up from time to time in the great landscaped parks of eighteenth-century Europe, but never on the scale of these.*

The most refined example must be the wall decorations in the Pompeiian manner for the drawing room, conceived and painted with the utmost finesse by one of the many foreign talents engaged on the royal building projects, the French artist and designer Louis Masreliez. These are Pompeiian in the late eighteenth-century understanding of that style, the strong colours and spatial games (walls painted to suggest several planes simultaneously) of the original frescoes tidied and simplified into elegant decorative schemes based on panels of figures framed in decorated borders. Characteristically, the figures – usually of classical deities, nymphs and so forth – are vividly coloured and grouped on a light background. Floral garlands, swags, fluttering cupids add to the delicate prettiness of the whole. Masreliez uses a dark colour, a *sang-de-boeuf* exactly matching the superb porphyry chimneypiece, for the borders decorated with grotesques which frame and anchor all this ethereality, but punctuates them with pale blue-and-white roundels in gilt frames which pick up, at dado height, the pale blue frieze with its procession of small classical figures and chimaera in grisaille. This pale blue frieze then modulates into the pale silk covers of gilded sofas. Masreliez – who also designed most of the Haga Pavilion furniture – was an exceptionally gifted decorator/designer in the same league as Robert Adam, and this room merits comparison with the Etruscan Room at Osterley Park, near London, for its charm of colouring and delicacy of execution, while retaining something of the intimate feeling of a drawing room in a small country house.

This detail of the Pompeiian-style decoration in the Haga drawing room gives some idea of the exceptional delicacy and skill of the designer and painter, Louis Masreliez, who was responsible for the decoration of the Pavilion. Every inch, from the continuous Greek key motif to the tiny roundels after della Robbia of embracing cherubs, is executed with meticulous care and finish. Note how Masreliez has matched the background colour of the small inset panels to the magnificent chimneypiece of Swedish porphyry. The gilding on mouldings and fillets in this scheme is of equally high quality. Scandinavian craftsmen have always been particularly expert gilders.

The Pompeiian drawing-room at the Haga Pavilion. The frescoed wall decorations from Pompeii, which were being excavated and to some extent published throughout the latter part of the eighteenth century, were a revelation to architects, designers and craftsmen of the day. One of the first important examples of the style in Europe was the Grand Salon of Marie-Antoinette's Petits Appartements at Versailles. It is likely that Gustav III, as well as his French decorator, had seen these, or at least, sketches of them. Gustav corresponded with the French Queen, and their tastes in furniture and decoration were similarly fastidious and fashion-conscious. Nymphs, candelabra and floral garlands framed in panels of grotesques, and executed in a wide colour palette, are features of the Pompeiian style, which differed from the so-called Etruscan style (later found to be late classical Greek, properly speaking) chiefly in its colouring. Etruscan rooms, inspired by black- and red-figure vases, were painted largely in red, black and white, with figures of a more exotic mythological pedigree such as harpies, sphinxes, griffins and lions. Masreliez's inspired contribution to the Pompeiian decorative style is the use of delicate blue and white.

ABOVE *Classical figures painted in grisaille on pure gold leaf, an overall scheme of white and gold interspersed with mirrored panels, and antique columns of real marble brought back from Italy, together form the decorative elements Masreliez used to conjure up a setting worthy of the Swedish Apollo; the grisaille technique is exquisite.*

Passing through a smaller anteroom, one reaches the grand finale, the *coup de théâtre* of Gustav's private pleasure dome, the Mirrored Drawing Room, a shimmering fantasy in white and gold as ravishing and delusive as one of the transparencies Louis Desprez designed for the Court Theatre at Drottningholm. The theatrical allusion is appropriate here because the astonishing end wall of this miniature Hall of Mirrors, its six marble columns lending substance to what is virtually a transparent wall of glass, is a daring invention even in an age of glass skyscrapers; in its own day it must have seemed sensationally sophisticated. Because columns and glazing were cut off at a floor level raised a few feet above the grassy slope to the lake, the whole glittering, refracting mirrored space seems to be floating out through the landscape towards the water, on a spectacular *Embarquement à Cythère*.

But the heroine of this *mise en scène*, framed in marble and mysteriously prolonged in the immense mirrored wall panels (which Gustav did not live to see completed), is Nature, spreading a lake almost at one's feet, and offering vistas of great trees where the slow round of the seasons could be contemplated in civilized comfort. A Nature kempt and re-arranged, but significantly, thoroughly Scandinavian in its juxtaposition of forest and water. It is interesting to note that the celebrated modern Louisiana Museum, outside Copenhagen, has glass walls opening out onto water, an arrangement which might well have been inspired by this magical eighteenth-century room.

Gustav liked to think of himself as Apollo, the sun god, and his mirrored room is, among other things, a Scandinavian temple of light. The decoration, also by Masreliez, is predominantly and appropriately golden. Groups of classical figures, painted in grisaille, stand out like shadows against panels of pure gold leaf at each end of the room, and the wall mirrors (made up of sheets exactly matched in size to window glass) are separated by rich but delicate decorative panels, painted white, with neo-classical ornament picked out in gold. Continuing the classical theme, gilded 'klysmos' chairs and sofas, also designed by Masreliez, line the walls, and a pair of marble urns stand on the ceramic pedestal stoves. Notably, the ceiling here, as throughout the Pavilion, is white and unadorned other than by glittering and beautiful chandeliers.

OPPOSITE *The entrancing and delusive reflectiveness of the Mirrored Drawing Room is well suggested by this view of the mirrored wall reflecting a series of tall windows opposite. Pier glasses between the windows, with pedestal stoves before them, prolong the reflective game. Gilded decoration on the wall panels uses an Etruscan vocabulary – gryphons, chimera, urns. The superb 'klysmos' chairs and sofas with their striped silk covers and radiant gilding were designed by Masreliez especially for this room. The huge mirrors are made up of separate mirrored panels of exactly the same size as the glass panes fitted into the 'glass' wall at the far end.*

Gustav must have had the Hall of Mirrors at Versailles in mind when he erected this extraordinary room, but it must be said that his dramatic wall of glass is a stroke of poetic invention which outstrips the original. Six antique marble columns, below a gilded frieze of classical deities, support a 'transparency' of glass panes set into an almost invisible bronze framework. This was a constructional tour de force in the 1780s, and a spectacular effect even today. Allusions are set up to classical Greek temples on the one hand, and to Gustav's beloved Court Theatre at Drottningholm, with its wave machines and scenic effects on the other. The floor, sliced cleanly across the base of the columns at a carefully judged level, gives the illusion of dissolving into the lake water beyond. If the room suggests an auditorium, the experience unfolded to a contemplative spectator is of change, growth and decay in an idealized natural world of clear lake water overhung by trees. Though carefully orchestrated by Gustav's landscape designer, this combination of trees and water is quintessentially Swedish and a reminder that Gustav III was a patriot in his fashion, appreciating the character and beauty of his country with the eye of a connoisseur. Just visible on the left is one of the pedestal stoves, surrounded by marble urns, which were used to heat the Mirrored Drawing Room, and designed to be fuelled and maintained from outside by unseen menials.

The decoration of the dining room of the Haga Pavilion is considerably more restrained – even austere – than the rest of Gustav's pleasure dome. In a quieter vein, it is however just as impressive and sophisticated, judged as a decorative ensemble. The dominant colours are grey, (pearl grey is the Gustavian colour) stone and bronze. Above a dado spattered in granite colours the walls are lightly marbled and painted to suggest relief carving. Splendid serving tables of neo-classical inspiration stand between the French windows on either side of the room, with marble-topped buffets on either side of the double doors from the adjacent vestibule. Presiding over the room, at the opposite end from the vestibule, is a towering ceramic stove of superbly chaste design, balanced by tall 'bronze' painted doors on either side. This cool, light, elegant room expresses a different strand of neo-classical taste, a certain gravitas reminiscent of Adam's great halls at Syon and Kedleston, but the use of painted effects recalls a very different, and later, building, Sir John Soane's bath house for Wimpole, in Cambridgeshire.

This detail emphasizes the extreme subtlety of the colours and paint effects used to decorate the Haga dining room. The dado shows how sophisticated spatter painting can look in the tones of grey granite. The trompe-l'oeil work above, in creamy stone colours, is unobtrusive but adds architectural weight and dignity to the ensemble. Tall doors, of native Swedish pine, are painted in a rich but muted bronze colour exactly matched to the pairs of bronze hinges. The subdued metallic glow of this finish was probably achieved by painting glazes in various colours over a reflective metallic base – metal leaf, or bronze powder.

If the Mirrored Drawing Room is the most thrilling and audacious of the Haga interiors, the comparatively sober dining room at the opposite end of the ground floor, long, tall and windowed along both sides, is interesting for its subtle use of low-key paint effects. The overall colouring of the room is the distinctive cool silvery grey which rapidly became a hallmark of the Gustavian style. The walls below dado level are spattered in subdued mauve/brown/grey to suggest – distantly – granite, an example of a simple technique made aristocratic. Immense panelled doors are finished in imitation of bronze, a paint effect favoured for its antique air during this period, but also used to disguise the fact that the doors are of pine rather than the figured mahogany commonly favoured in great houses, such as Adam's Kenwood, in London, or, nearer home, in Copenhagen's Dehn Palœ. Dramatically overscaled serving tables are likewise painted in pearl grey, lightly glazed to give them an antique look. But the dramatic feature of the dining room, unquestionably, is an immense white ceramic stove in the purest classical idiom, a column set on a pedestal, which towers almost to the ceiling between a pair of bronzed doors. Because of its sophisticated restraint and the bold scale of its furnishings, this room feels surprisingly modern – or perhaps post-modern, given its neo-classical pedigree.

Gustav III spent several fortunes on rare and beautiful, or simply pretty and ingenious, objects with which to ornament the rooms at the Haga Pavilion. Such connoisseurship was an understandable foible in a collector of so informed and fastidious a taste, but tactical folly for a monarch who had just involved his country in a costly and unsuccessful Russian campaign. The King's extravagance must have been a factor in the mounting rebelliousness among the Swedish nobles, which exploded into violence during a masked ball at the Stockholm Opera, where Captain Jacob Johan Anckarström, from one of Sweden's oldest families, shot the King in the back at point-blank range. Instead of bullets the assassin used rusty nails, in the knowledge that if the shot failed to kill, any wound would become gangrenous, and thereby fatal. Which is what in fact happened; Gustav died thirteen days later on March 29, 1792, having endured great suffering with fortitude. The tiny upstairs powder closet where Gustav's valet powdered his master's hair before the ball is much as it was then, simply furnished, its smallness emphasized by a ceramic stove looming out of the far corner, the top almost touching the ceiling, and the walls lined with painted canvas decorated with an ornamental fillet.

The closet is one of a succession of captivating rooms on the Pavilion's top storey which provided accommodation for the King's valet, the Crown Prince and his tutor, and a guest. Gustav's own bedchamber is on the ground floor, decorated and furnished considerably more lavishly, with silk brocade lining the walls and draping the alcove bed. By comparison, the attic rooms, reached by a narrow staircase contained in the thickness of a wall, are treated frugally, in much the same style as the powder closet, but each one with a different motif for the ornamental painted fillets which subdivide the walls into 'panels', and with different, modest, sprigged fabrics curtaining their alcove beds. For one reason or another, their intimate scale, or their touching simplicity, these small chambers are deeply atmospheric, especially in the late afternoon when the sun sinks behind the trees outside the small square windows. A modern visitor can more easily imagine these rooms occupied, the valet busying about the life-sized dummies where a choice of clothes were displayed for the King to choose from for the following day, a guest checking his reflection in the pretty gilt mirror lit by two candles, the Crown Prince's tutor reading in a comfortable *fauteuil* (more generously cushioned and inviting than the formal suites of furniture downstairs) by the stove. It seems almost certain that this floor was for men only. There is a story, plausible in the light of what was known and written about Gustav's habits, that his wife, Sophia Maddalena, paid a visit unannounced to the Pavilion on one occasion, and was so scandalized by the scenes of revelry she found there that she departed immediately, never to return. The King's sister-in-law, Hedvig Charlotta, Duchess of Södermanland, denounced the Haga and its lifestyle as more suited 'to the twelve Caesars . . . than a Christian king'.

After Gustav's untimely death, a predictable and censorious reaction set in against the pleasure-loving King and his legacy of dazzling but extravagant buildings. The ravishing Court Theatre at Drottningholm gradually decayed, the huge stockpile of stone, marble and other imported building materials destined for the Haga Palace (it was to have cost two million sterling, an unthinkable sum in those days) went towards building the War Academy for military cadets, while the Haga Pavilion received the philistine treatment so often meted out to idiosyncratic masterpieces; the furnishings were dispersed among other royal residences (identifiable, and recoverable however, due to a code mark stamped on each piece), the remarkable book collection in the King's white and gold library was auctioned off, the first or mezzanine floor was partially destroyed and, final indignity, the exquisite wall decorations by Masreliez and his team were covered with safe, respectable damask. At least they were not overpainted, as were many of the interiors in the Court Theatre. The damask probably helped preserve them.

Two centuries later, Gustav III's reputation has been rehabilitated. Selfish, extravagant and irresponsible, he was not what is normally thought of as a 'good king'; no one could have been more different from old Gustavus Vasa, the father of his people, who wrote to his wife as 'hustru', lived frugally, governed craftily, and left Sweden more united, powerful and prosperous than he had found it. On the other

This modest, small, low-ceilinged garret is the most historically interesting of all the rooms in the Haga Pavilion. It was Gustav III's dressing room, or powder closet, and it was in here that the king's valet dressed his master for the masked ball at the Stockholm Opera where Anckharström, the leader of a nobles' conspiracy, shot him in the back with a pistol loaded with rusty nails, a striking and tragic scene which Verdi seized upon as a subject for his opera, Un Ballo in Maschera.

hand, the later Gustav founded the Swedish Academy, was an enlightened and generous patron of all the arts, and a brilliant, sophisticated individual with the perspicacity, taste and energy to breathe new confidence and purpose into Sweden's cultural life, to admit and try new aesthetic ideas, whether in stage design, landscape art, interior decoration or architecture. More than any other Swedish king, before or since, he tried to make his countrymen feel part of Europe, in the mainstream instead of a backwater. And in the Haga Pavilion he created a pearl among palaces. When the dull damask was removed and the painted decoration cleaned and restored, the Haga was able to shine once more as the most polished example of a decorative style, poised, limpid, harmonious, which may have owed something to classical Greece and Rome, but has since come to seem essentially Scandinavian.

Drottningholm Court Theatre

Hidden away like an incomparably pretty trinket in the bosom of the Drottningholm Court Theatre, the tiny single-windowed boudoir and dressing room reserved for the leading actress or *prima donna* (Gustav III staged Mozart operas, as well as the plays which he wrote, produced or performed in whenever state business permitted) is a place which wraps up certain elements special to Scandinavian style in one delectable little package. The whole room is not much more than four metres square. Apart from a pretty marble fireplace surround (real this time) its furnishings can never have been much more elaborate than they are now, chiefly useful tables for wig stands and making up, plus a little sofa for resting on during the intervals and one or two chairs for visitors and dressers. The floor is bare, the bleached boards which feature so regularly throughout the north. In its modesty of means and decorative flair, plus a touch of sweet disorder intriguingly evocative of backstage life, it is altogether a *femme fatale* of a room.

A generous rush-seated chair, real marble chimneypiece and pewtery old mirrorglass add up to a handsomely informal corner from one of the bedrooms at the Drottningholm Court Theatre. This one, with alcove bed, was used by the architect while the theatre was being decorated and completed around him. The panel to the right of the fireplace shows the original eighteenth-century wall finish, much more lavishly decorated with floral ropes, which was hidden beneath later layers of coloured distemper edged by printed paper borders. Sun streams in through the immense floor-to-ceiling windows of this odd blend of private hotel and theatre.*

Pretty but dilapidated furniture, another pretty mirror, and a utilitarian row of wooden pegs fill up an entire wall of the ravishing painted tapeter, *showing giant peonies and exotic birds on a scale which dwarfs this tiny room to splendid effect.*

ABOVE *This detail from the corner furthest from the window, and thus least faded, gives some idea of the brilliance of the original colours – pinks, green and browns with flashes of coloured plumage.*

Of course the magic is explicable; anyone with half an eye can see that it is all done with paint, to be specific, painted canvas (or possibly canvas-backed paper) representations of a gnarled little oriental (magnolia, tree paeony?) tree hung with immense flowers and buds in colours ranging from coral (in the corner furthest from the light) to a pale rose whose artist's equivalent can only be *cuisse de nymphe*. Long-tailed birds, their exotic plumage tactfully faded to match, perch decoratively on convenient twigs. The canvas panels are stitched or, rather, cobbled together with twine, now visible here and there like Herrick's 'erring laces', and the top and bottom edges are secured by a profusion of rusty nails, as indeed early printed papers were before some bright individual thought of pasting them down invisibly. None of this detracts from the ensemble in the least; if anything, this rude handling of a ravishing scenic prop adds to its charm. The flowering, bird-hung tree is absurdly overscaled in a room where it seems that a tall man must stoop, but this, too, is part of the secret of the Prima Donna's Dressing Room. Scandinavia's dolls'-house rooms furnished with life-sized pieces return one to childhood, to a Wonderland far more consoling than Alice's. They must make everyone want to revise their ideas of suitably decorating tiny rooms. Normally, the tree motif shown here would have been displayed above the dado in a room of respectable height and dimensions, the sort of room which French châteaux frequently treated to a similarly feminine and delectable form of decoration. The magic touch, probably fortuitous in the light of their endearingly frequent gaffes, lay in using such a boldly scaled motif not just here and there but consecutively, insistently, right round a painted hatbox of a room.

RIGHT *The chimneypiece is of carved stone with a sizeable stone hearth before it. A good open fire would have been quite adequate to warm such a small place. The canvas-backed tapeter is nailed, sagging a little, to the walls below a simple coving.*

ABOVE *A vignette from one of Drottningholm's many passages and galleries.*

The late John Fowler, who knew a brilliant decorative stroke when he saw it, and was particularly susceptible, in his prescient way, to the Scandinavian alliance of extreme sophistication with poignant simplicity, imitated this particularly memorable motif in a little garden pavilion he designed for Lady Diana Duff-Cooper. Against walls colourwashed in a glowing apricot/terracotta he re-interpreted, using the same scale, the Drottningholm Tree of Heaven, in grisaille, chalky pale against subdued colour, with equally, but differently, ravishing effect. This might be taken as an object lesson by anyone who wonders whether new wine can be justifiably decanted into old bottles. The answer, surely, as in any branch of creative effort, is, yes, provided one seizes upon the essential character of the thing-that-inspires, the quiddity of the thing, and goes beyond lifeless imitation towards a new, personal replay.

The Drottningholm Court Theatre is, itself, something of an architectural sport, a private royal amusement park where an unusually civilized monarch revelled in creating, with help from his protégés, theatrical experiences which would astonish, charm, and perhaps elevate his somewhat chauvinistic courtiers. The wonderfully effective stage machinery which survives shows just how ardently Gustav espoused this particular role of magician, provider of spectacle. There are wind machines which howl, thunder and lightning effects that flash and boom so that one clutches one's seat, and an especially delightful and realistic wave-simulating machine, where undulating painted canvas flaps revolve hypnotically on rollers cranked by a single handle. The Prima Donna's Dressing Room, thoughtfully, is a hop and a skip from the stage, its tiny door almost hidden by stage machinery. Lesser fry had further to go, before they could unbutton, throw off their wigs, and relax. If the past, theirs and ours, seems close beneath the skin of everyday life in Scandinavia, the flavour that comes through at Drottningholm is pungently eighteenth century, and its bright, insouciant little heart, like the glowing remnant of the Tin Soldier's dancer love in Hans Andersen's touching fable, is the delicately gaudy and fantastical dressing room pictured here.

OPPOSITE *The far end of the architect's room shown on page 208 shows a pretty checked bed looking somewhat dwarfed by its towering alcove. The original eighteenth-century bed might well have been taller and more imposing. The jib door at left connects with a small washroom.*

STENINGE MANOR

The Scandinavian practice of distributing various family activities through a series of separate buildings, which runs through every social level from farmhouses upwards, is given forceful architectural expression at Steninge, the country house built by Tessin the Younger for Carl Gyllenstierna. Gyllenstierna was the favourite of the Dowager Queen Hedvig Eleonora, who made him Governor of her household as well as the manager of her estates. Hedvig Eleonora was fourteen years older than Gyllenstierna, and by the time Steninge was completed in 1699 their association had lasted over thirty years. Whether their relationship went deeper than friendship can only be a matter for speculation. They were neither of them young by the turn of the century. However it would be interesting to know how contemporaries reacted to the news that permanent accommodation for the Queen was provided at Steninge, in the shape of a separate pavilion, known as the Queen's Wing, as well as a state room in the main house 'in case it should please her Royal Majesty to stay.' The Queen interested herself closely in the design, building and decoration of the manor house and its wings, and her old-fashioned tastes for the heavier style of baroque seem to have set the tone for many of the interiors. Externally the group of three buildings, linked by formal gardens in the Italian manner, and facing out across Lake Mälaren, are painted a warm peach colour, the unostentatious but dignified façade of the main house enriched with busts and statues in niches. All three buildings have the *sateri*, or mansard roof, which would go out of fashion later in the eighteenth century.

Viewed from the bottom of wide steps carpeted heavily with snow, the front elevation of Steninge, painted in vivid peachy-ochre and white, stands out warmly against a wintry sky and leafless trees. It was built at the turn of the seventeenth century by Sweden's leading architect of the day, Tessin the Younger, for a royal favourite, Carl Gyllenstierna.

ABOVE *Trompe-l'oeil bands of 'guilloches' in dull blue on gold skilfully suggest low-relief carved decoration around painted doorways at Steninge. It has been suggested that carving coniferous softwoods proved so difficult and unsatisfactory that local craftsmen were driven to find other ways of creating opulent effects, becoming exceptionally skilled at all the minor* illusionmålning *devices, such as the one shown here. Work of this standard was always slow, and therefore reserved for the mansions of the rich aristocracy.*

Though Steninge was completed by 1700, its official housewarming, attended by the Queen and also Johan Harleman, who laid out the garden, was not held till 1705. The following year Gyllenstierna made what appears to have been a prudent rather than romantic marriage to another rich widow, with the plebeian-sounding name of Anna Maria Soop. Possibly to reassure his bride that the Dowager Queen, now in her fifties, would not interfere in the running of Steninge, Gyllenstierna made the place over to her as a wedding present. Hedvig died in 1715, and Gyllenstierna eight years later, after which Steninge eventually passed into the possession of Count Axel von Fersen, 'le beau Fersen', whose involvement with Marie-Antoinette was to make him a romantic legend. A Sèvres coffee set which Marie-Antoinette gave Fersen is still on display in the house.

The oval drawing room, or great salon, is one of the most impressive baroque interiors in the grand style in Sweden. With its rich tones of marbling, in shades of crimson and maroon, and elaborately decorated domed ceiling, lavishly picked out in gold leaf, it has a family resemblance to some of the contemporary interiors at Drottningholm, where Hedvig Eleanora lived. Even the marbling, both in colour and style, is reminiscent of Drottingholm's double staircase and entrance hall. Restored early this century, the *marmorering* nevertheless has the oldness of baroque work; the modulation between the dark rich reds with ochreish veining and a cool grey-brown marbling in between is sumptuous and dignified. A set of Italian statues, of white marble, was acquired during the last century to fill the round-headed niches set at intervals round the walls, flanked by marbled pilasters. Though a little out of keeping with the baroque spirit of the room, they stand out dramatically from their dark surrounds, and the presence of so many life-size lightly draped nymphs and goddesses certainly adds drama and animation to the overall effect.

RIGHT *A number of different specimens of faux marble are shown in this detail from the oval salon at Steninge. While skilful and painterly, it is noteworthy that the 'faux' marbles are decorative in intention rather than geologically exact. The white marble figures in wall niches are nineteenth-century additions. It would be interesting to discover what the niches held originally.*

An overview of the oval salon showing more of the thirteen varieties of faux marble used in this decoration (black on the chimneypiece, blond on walls) as well the immense chandelier which is the coruscating centrepiece of an intensely decorated and colourful domed ceiling. The amethyst/claret shades which dominate the decoration are an unusual choice, especially in Scandinavia. They have been followed through with care, in damask seat covers as well as the floral carpet in Aubusson style.

LEFT *Scandinavian love of symmetry is demonstrated by a handsomely decorated pair of doors surmounted by niches containing marble urns, from the Dowager Queen's Pavilion at Steninge. Even in the cold blue light of a Swedish winter the gold leaf lavished on door panels contrives to glow cheerfully.*

ABOVE *Though decorated ceilings were a feature of Scandinavian seventeenth- and early eighteenth-century interiors, they were rarely as ambitious as the elaborately painted vault above the Oval Salon. This is conceived in the grand manner of European painted decoration, with bright floral garlands looped across demi-lune arches opening onto glimpses of blue painted sky with wispy cloud.*

LEFT *Rich gold leaf combined with* trompe-l'oeil *is a striking feature of the decoration of Steninge. The blue paint is characteristic of so many Swedish interiors that one feels it should be designated by a particular name, such as Baltic blue.*

TUREHOLMS GÅRD

In 1719 Russian troops landed on Sweden's east coast and ravaged the countryside, looting and burning several old manor houses and castles in their path. One of these was Tureholms, at that time the property of the aristocratic Bielke family. Like their neighbours and fellow-victims at Sandemar and Beatelund, the Bielke family re-built on the same site. They employed the Swedish architect, Carl Hårleman, who was one of the most successful designers of his day, responsible for the chapel to the new Royal Palace in Stockholm, and the austerely hand-some East India Company headquarters in Gothenburg. Though Har-leman had recently visited France to study the latest buildings, his design for Tureholms was firmly based on the old baroque building which had stood there previously even to the extent of incorporating some of the remaining walls. This preference for building in earlier styles is typical of much Swedish architecture of the seventeenth and eighteenth centuries. It is quite possible that the conservatism implied was on the part of the clients, who saw no reason to depart from estab-lished models, rather than of the architects.

Externally, Tureholms as it is today is a tall ochre-washed building, detailed in white, with detached pavilions. The house is reached up a long sloping ramp which in earlier times was the bridge over an encir-cling moat fed by the sea. By the time Tureholms came to be re-built, three hundred years after its predecessor, the sea level had fallen. Both the manor and its pavilions have the distinctive 'sateri' roof which gives such an attractive silhouette to the grander houses of the period. Sateri roofs slope down in two stages, usually with a short vertical section be-tween. At Tureholms the vertical 'waistband' is studded with round gilded ornaments. The sateri style is said to derive from the chalet-type

Few Scandinavian interiors are as unexpected or captivating as the whimsical rococo chinoiserie 'kitchen' tucked away in the stony bulk of Tureholms Gård. More boudoir than kitchen, fashioned for aristocratic Swedish ladies, this egregious room was fitted out and decorated in the mid-eighteenth century to serve a double purpose. It was designed as a display cabinet for *the Bielke family's exceptional collection of Chinese blue-and-white porcelain, while also providing an original setting for the tea parties then beginning to infiltrate social life across Europe. The charming decorations, clearly patterned on the porcelain design, cover the walls, doors and built-in cupboards with a willow-pattern panorama of palms, pagodas and humpbacked bridges.*

ABOVE *This detail from the wall-hangings shown opposite, in the first floor salon, suggests the type of blue-and-white porcelain which the Bielke family might have displayed in the rococo kitchen.*

roof, which may be technically correct, but gives a misleading impression of something quite small scale. Some of the largest and grandest country houses, like Sturefors, and Steninge, have *sateri* roofs, their stepped outline giving a certain sprightliness to otherwise severely restrained elevations. It is possible that these roofs were structurally stronger, and better able to carry the extra weight of winter snow.

According to Tureholms' present owner, who lives in one of the pavilions, the building was reconstructed in locally made brick, but a good deal of stone was used internally, for floors at ground level, and for staircases. Many of the first-floor rooms are hung with painted hangings thought to be the work of a Swedish decorative painter called Mandelberg. The strangest of these is an early example of *chinoiserie* executed in darkly glowering colours which may have been suggested by old oriental lacquer. The hangings are in serious need of restoration, their surfaces 'alligatoring' badly, but the general effect is still handsome and colourful, against deep blue or green woodwork colours.

RIGHT *When* trompe-l'oeil *does not quite come off, the result, as here in a bedroom, can be positively surreal. Busts, urns, a statue holding a lyre, beribboned garlands and pairs of columns are all useful* trompe-l'oeil *devices but swamped by restless marbling and acanthus scrolls.*

The rather sombre colouring of chinoiserie decoration in the salon – possibly due to discolouration of the crusty varnish – is admirably set off, however, by paintwork of flat, thundery blue. Brightly coloured parakeets, curly eaves and oddly clad figures with pigtails combine with porcelain garnitures to suggest the allure of the mysterious East in a style which Sir William Chambers christened with the charming name of 'sharawaggi'.

But the pearl of Tureholms, decoratively speaking, is the extraordinary blue-and-white rococo 'kitchen' on the ground floor. The painting here is definitely credited to Mandelberg, and it has something of the awkwardness that characterizes the style of the hangings, here displayed to advantage in enchantingly naïve wall decorations based on the blue-and-white scenery of Chinese export porcelain, complete with trees, tiny pagodas, gowned sages with funny pointed hats, and waving palm fronds. An exotic effect rather than a literal transposition of china painting motifs was Mandelberg's aim, and the result is a triumphant one-off, with a blend of the fantastic and the homely which is at once distinctively Scandinavian, and irresistible.

The reason for calling it a 'kitchen', in quotation marks, is that it was not intended to be used for serious cooking; the real manor kitchens lay elsewhere, to the rear of the building. This blue-and-white kitchen was a *jeu d'esprit* on the lines of the exotic summerhouses and garden pavilions then becoming fashionable, only, and wisely in view of the prevailing climate, transported indoors. It was commissioned by the Countess Bielke of the day, as an original setting for the display of an immense and valuable collection of blue-and-white Chinese porcelain; a setting which could be used, moreover, for entertaining other ladies to the fashionable and novel tea ritual. A large open fireplace on the left of the room was used both for heating the room, and for baking little cakes and brewing up tea.

The china was displayed in two ways, in themselves a fascinating juxtaposition of high style and rustic tradition. High style – surely suggested by Daniel Marot's seventeenth-century engravings of porcelain 'cabinets' – suggested perching the smaller pieces, handleless cups and small bottles and jars, on small plaster brackets moulded in the shape of winged cherub's heads. These – alas now minus their pretty cups, the whole collection having long since been dispersed – stud whole stretches of wall, a large cluster above the door, above a dresser on the opposite wall, and ringing the mirror on the window wall. Each little cherub is carefully painted and picked out in the same deep but transparent blue (imitating the china colour) used for all the painted decorations. The rustic, even peasant, element in the room is contributed by built-in shelving ranging all the way up the walls to the ceiling. The shelves have sensible rails to prevent large pieces sliding off, or toppling forward, and they must once have housed a prodigious collection of blue-and-white plates and serving dishes. Shelves like these can be seen built into peasant cottages, also to display plates and china, but not painted as Mandelberg's are, with a tiny decorative motif running along all the leading edges. Careful touches like this add immensely to the charm of the room.

Delicate blue-and-white marbling in the kolmard style links panels of chinoiserie *decoration on the window embrasures in the rococo kitchen. Notice how the cherubic wall brackets, of painted plaster, form a wreath around a gilt pier glass. The floor of local slate in a mysterious purple-brown shade has worn away dramatically to a texture like pumice stone. An immense open fireplace and a small bread oven take up the width of the wall opposite the windows.*

Scenes from the sharawaggi world alternate with wispy marbling over this corner of the same kitchen. The colour scheme is simple but immensely effective – shades of Prussian blue with the cool silvery white obtained with lead white.

Even the shelf fronts have their own strip of painted decoration, showing up clearly in this detail. Despite drooping moustaches and an exotic castellated bonnet the Chinaman taking tea in the background looks stubbornly European, if not Swedish.

The overall style of this playful kitchen-cum-display cabinet, is spiritedly eclectic, rococo decoration being used to enhance a china collection of the sort which was all the rage during the period. The marbling, loosely swirled across panelling and provincial-style commode, is in the light-handed rococo style which was also used on church pews and smaller painted items. The decoration must have been conceived some time after the reconstruction of Tureholms, probably towards the middle of the eighteenth century. One can then imagine the then Countess Bielke, addicted to tea parties and blue-and-white china, having a sudden inspiration to create a room which would accommodate both, gracefully as became an extra boudoir, but at the same time, sensibly. All the same, one cannot help wondering how many tiny fragile cups were broken as servants climbed to replace them on their charming cherub brackets.

None of the original furniture, apart from the decorated commode and mirror above, remains. The floor, of native slate in a mauve/brown characteristic of that part of Sweden (the hall at Beatelund is paved with it too), is deeply cracked and worn away, with a splendidly hoary texture. One piece of furniture which would have been indispensable, apart from sets of pretty chairs which one imagines might have been marbled in blue and white, is one of the special tables, with a decorated porcelain top resting on a wooden base (really a shallow sink) which were a fashionable adjunct to the tea ceremony, used by the hostess delicately to rinse the precious cups after use. Sometimes these were provided with a candleholder each side, usually in ormolu. Tables of this type now fetch enormous prices in sale rooms and antique shops, having improbably survived into the twentieth century.

Regrettable as it may be that one can no longer see this charmingly frivolous room complete with a massed display of whimsically decorated porcelain, it has to be said that in its present state one is much better able to enjoy and appreciate Mandelberg's lighthearted blue-and-white panorama, which must have been almost obliterated when every wall bracket held an ornament and the shelves were stacked with plates.

LISELUND

Liselund, on the Danish island of Møn, is generally acknowledged to be the pearl of Scandinavian summerhouses, a distinction due in part to its melodious name (it means 'Lisa's grove'), in part to its idyllic situation on the very margin of a wooded lake, but most of all to its captivating, idiosyncratic architecture. Its cool Quakerish exterior of whitewashed brick and trim thatch only serves to delay, and enhance, the surprise of painted interiors of butterfly brilliance and elegant frivolity where one finds lighthearted borrowings from Le Petit Trianon, from the Brighton Pavilion, from a whole fantastical family of aristocratic eighteenth-century adult play houses.

It is no surprise to find that Liselund was conceived of, planned and decorated by Frenchmen, albeit both naturalized Danes, for the use and pleasure of a young and pretty woman. Antoine de la Calmette, who built Liselund in 1793 for his Swiss wife, Elizabeth Iselin, nicknamed Lisa, was of French Huguenot extraction. His family, expelled from France following the persecutions of 1685, settled in various parts of Europe, finally taking root in Denmark, where his father found a niche in the diplomatic service while Antoine was still a boy. Antoine's father prospered, bought various properties in Denmark, and brought his children up as Danes. Antoine inherited on his father's death in 1781, and subsequently married Lisa, the daughter of a Swiss banker and herself a considerable heiress. Shortly after, he embarked on the creation of a summerhouse which would be at once a graceful tribute to his bride, and a playful repository of the fashionable ideas and cosmopolitan tastes formed by a much-travelled childhood, his own natural inclination, and the sort of permeability to learned enthusiasms so characteristic of educated eighteenth-century aristocrats. The result is sometimes, rather as with the Brighton Pavilion, a salad of styles. A Chinese fretwork motif in *trompe-l'oeil* on the dado, for instance, meets up with Pompeiian-style grotesques in grisaille above. But there is no feeling of *mésalliance*. The colours are so artful and pretty, the execution so lively and skilful that the general effect is rather of an exuberant invention regulated by a cultivated taste and eye.

Whitewash and thatch applied to wooden columns and a frivolous bell tower add up to a delightful hybrid of a summerhouse, part pleasure pavilion or lusthus, *part 'rustic' cottage, part decorative folly, one of a family dotted about Liselund's romantic parkland by the sea.*

229

Architecturally, Liselund is something of a hybrid, at once a proper summerhouse in the Scandinavian tradition of a second summer home, and a sort of composite of two types of building that found favour in the latter part of the eighteenth century, the cottage ornée and the pleasure pavilion, which in Scandinavia becomes a *lusthus*. Outwardly the cottage analogy prevails; the deep thatch, with round scoops for dormer windows, makes this plain, though a tiny bell tower and a simple but classical colonnaded verandah (this must be a rare instance of a thatched roof supported on columns) indicate that this cottage is more rustick than rustic. The small size and scale of Liselund are also consonant with a cottage theme; while larger than any of the authentic thatched cottages found in most Danish villages, it remains a small house.

The architect of Liselund was Andreas Kirkerup, Court Architect of his day. But this is one house where the decorator's talents take centre stage. The interiors are the work of Danish Court painter J.C. Lillie, whose name proclaims his French extraction. Lillie, on the evidence of his work at Liselund, was a designer of considerable taste and versatility, with a catholic sensibility which allowed him to mix fashionable high-style elements with traditional, even folky, Scandinavian effects, all with grace, wit and aplomb. Undoubtedly too, Liselund provides a case of patron and the artist finding themselves in perfect accord. Lillie designed all the furniture, of painted softwood in the Scandinavian manner popularized by Gustav III of Sweden, in an eclectic mixture of fashionable styles ranging from Louis Seize to Hepplewhite; he also designed the delicate and charming mirrors with tiny wall-hung matching console tables. Framed, or hung with carved and painted floral swags, these are a conspicuous feature of this most elegant of summerhouses. But he was also capable of realizing relatively sober schemes, such as the bedroom painted in Pompeiian red; against this the painted 'bois clair' furniture, a tented *lit duchesse*, and two remarkable *trompe-l'oeil* closet doors, showing Grecian urns filled with informal bouquets and standing on curious tripod tables with claw feet, stand out with theatrical impact.

Lillie clearly enjoyed thinking up decorative schemes which contained playful allusions to the personal history of his patron, Antoine de la Calmette. The 'monkey room', for instance, is dominated by a mirrored panel framed by painted palms (reminiscent of the Brighton Pavilion kitchen) and decorated with a painted trapeze on which a devilish little monkey is perched. The presence of the monkey in this wonderfully eclectic scheme goes back to a dramatic incident in Antoine de la Calmette's early childhood, when his father was living in Lisbon. One night when Antoine would have been about seven or eight, he was woken by the screams and chattering of a frightened monkey, presumably a family pet, since monkeys are not indigenous to Portugal. What the animal had sensed, long before his human hosts, was the onset of the massive earthquake which devastated Lisbon in 1755. His monkey alarm evidently saved the little boy's life, and years later was gratefully recorded in the lively, if anatomically dubious, furry homunculus which presides, arm outstretched and tail dangling, over one of the most impish neo-classical painted interiors to have survived into the twentieth century.

Like so many other architectural survivals, Liselund owes its preservation to neglect following financial collapse rather than any officious intention to keep it whole and in a proper state of repair. It is one of the ironies of history that the most perfect interiors salvaged from earlier centuries have reached us intact not because anyone took pains to ensure their preservation but because subsequent owners, or inhabitants, were too poor to even contemplate repairs, let alone what later generations invariably designate as 'improvements'.

In the case of Liselund, the property passed to a spendthrift son, Charles de la Calmette, whose first act of rebellion was to insist on marrying the local doctor's daughter, Martha Meckeprang, in the teeth of fierce family opposition. Then, on the death of his parents, he proceeded, in the time-honoured fashion of spoilt elder sons, to squander the family fortunes in the space of a few years. When he died, prematurely, Liselund, its contents and the estate were sold up, but with the (generous) proviso that Charles' widow could continue to live there for her lifetime. She lived for another fifty-seven years, which must have been a test of forbearance on the part of the new owner, Gottlob Rosenkranz. Her own limited means, together with a sentimental regard for the home into which she had married, meant that the doctor's daughter left Liselund untouched during her half century of tenure, a period (the 1820s to 1870s) when any other house of this calibre would normally have undergone frequent and radical decorative facelifts. (The ravishing interiors by Nash and Frederick Crace for the Brighton Pavilion, for instance, were buried under painted lincrusta or conventional stretched damask, while the scintillating collections of furniture and *objets de vertu* were dispersed, mainly into other Royal collections.)

After an interval during which the little pavilion became a sort of grace-and-favour house for various Danish artists, who relished and recorded its Grand Meaulnes atmosphere, Liselund has found a new devotee and patron in the present representative of the Rosenkranz family. Most unusually for a building of such an apparently fragile and frivolous character, Liselund retains almost every item and detail of its original decoration and furnishing, from stoves concealed with 'Etruscan' bronze urns, to garlanded console tables, Louis Seize 'bergères' in faded striped silk, and extraordinary, brilliant Empire pendant lamps of turquoise glass and ormolu. Anyone sensitive to atmosphere, and period, finds in Antoine de la Calmette's *nid d'amour* the double pleasure of a ravishing, whimsical variation on the neo-classical theme, and an extraordinarily complete encapsulation of a mode of existence which today seems only a little less remote and unimaginable than Pompeii, from which so many of its decorative schemes were borrowed.

The long drawing-room at Liselund, commanding views across the lake and the park, is painted simply but effectively in a soft pink framed by green borders. The Danes seem on the whole to have preferred paler pastel colours and simpler decorative schemes than their Scandinavian neighbours. It is the furniture which impresses here – the chandelier, a real crystal fountain, has the airy delicacy found in the native ornamental glass fittings. The stove, marred by an obtrusive black flue, is a classical version of the standard pattern, a pedestal of cast iron. The oval mirror, with its garlands and ribbon topknot, partnered by a tiny console table, completes this distinctively Nordic ensemble.

In the misty early morning light, the long drawing-room at Liselund has something almost aqueous about it, like the inside of a translucent shell. Sparsely furnished, other than by the irresistible view, this would have been a room for musical evenings, reading of poetry and other fashionable pastimes of the Age of Sensibility.

HEMBYGSGÅRDEN

From the late eighteenth century, two distinctively northern crops, flax and timber, made Sweden's Baltic province of Hålsingland, in the north-east, one of the most prosperous regions of the country. Such was the wealth of Hålsingland's peasant farmers and landowners that they thought nothing of celebrating family occasions such as christenings, weddings and name days with champagne and fine wines, thus distancing themselves from the *brannvin*-swilling lower orders. (*Brannvin*, or 'burnt wine', was a powerful liquor distilled from potatoes over which Gustav III held a lucrative royal monopoly.) As a permanent and visible mark of their new-found prosperity, they spent money on their homes, adding a second storey perhaps, a *herrstuga* or party house, or commissioning local painters to decorate rooms and furniture in the style of the day, as they knew it.

Hembygsgården, in the village of Edsbyn in Hålsingland is a remarkably intact monument to this palmy period in the fortunes of the Nilsson family of farmers and considerable landowners who have occupied it continuously for at least two hundred and fifty years. Nilsson family history, preserved through oral tradition, does not record the exact date when the Nilssons began living at Hembygsgården, but they were sufficiently established to embark on a programme of ambitious decoration by 1775 or thereabouts. The original *stuga* dates back to the sixteenth century and there is reason to suppose that Nilssons built it and lived in it from the first, and that it expanded along with their family fortunes.

Spotlit by frail winter sunshine, the entrance porch to Hembygsgården is in the rustic/classical style so common throughout Scandinavia, though there are some unusual flourishes, such as the frieze of diamond shaped cut-outs. A row of little panels above the double doors, attractively picked out in colour, *admits light to what must otherwise be an extremely dark hallway. Notice the casual way in which a window on the later second storey fails to line up with the centre of the porch. Rustic houses such as this tended to grow haphazardly and certainly without the benefit of architectural advice.*

A droll manikin, part cherub, part revelling Silenus, with blue wings, a spear and a fruit dish in his outstretched hand, gazes enquiringly out of a vaguely Italianate landscape in the stor stuga – or 'big room' – decorated by Jonas Hertman and his wife. The tiny shelf edged with tatted lace is one of many dotted about the walls to hold candlesticks on party nights.

Hembygsgården, as it now stands – and little or nothing in the property has been altered since the mid-nineteenth century – consists of three buildings finished with timber cladding, painted in Falun red, and dignified with handsome carved porches and doors in the regional style, painted white, and picked out in yellow, grey and green. The main house, or winter house, forms an open-ended courtyard together with the summer house on its right, and a large barn on its left. The barn was used for livestock, storage, and as – rudimentary – servants' quarters. The summer house was not so much a second holiday home, as the centre of the family's flax-into-linen production during the summer months, and its rooms are filled with spinning wheels and looms. But the important building to the Nilsson family, and the one on which they spent considerable sums of money, was the winter house, which has all the distinguishing features of prospering peasant taste. These included a second storey (added in 1820 or so), a *storstuga*, or 'big room' for partying, lavishly decorated, and a second, smaller parlour, probably intended for the women to withdraw to while the men grew boisterous over champagne in the party room. As in all homes of the *stuga* class, however, the heart of family life, where everyone foregathered in winter, was the kitchen. Formerly the kitchen was not only the communal living room, but also the dormitory, where everyone slept, though this traditional pattern of peasant life altered after the house grew a second storey.

The variety and intensity of painted decoration throughout Hembygsgården interiors is a characteristic feature of many old wooden cottages and houses in Hålsingland, a region famed for the vigour and colourfulness of its vernacular decorative tradition. Conservators in the area today often have difficulty persuading *stuga* owners of the need to maintain and preserve painted interiors which they take for granted because they see them on all sides. Yet this particular efflorescence of folk decoration is so tightly regional that the neighbouring province, Gastrikland, has very little to show of comparable quality.

Aside from its sheer exuberance, what makes the painted decoration at Hembygsgården so interesting is that, for once, something is known about the painter responsible for most of it, notably the ambitious murals in the 'big room'. His name was Jonas Hertman (1755–1804), a name which may indicate German ancestry, and he combined several trades in the struggle to provide for a wife and nine children. He farmed, like the Nilssons, but on a much smaller scale. He also made clocks. There are many vividly painted grandfather clocks at Hembygsgården, and it is possible that Jonas made and painted some of these. Sadly, for all his undoubted talent and versatility, Jonas Hertman failed to share in the burgeoning prosperity of his province, and died a pauper with little but debts to bequeath to his family, though the household inventory made at his death records that Jonas possessed a Bible illustrated with woodcuts as well as a hymnal. Like so many other largely self-taught Scandinavian vernacular artists he would have drawn heavily on the Bible illustrations for themes and motifs for his mural work. His wife often accompanied him and helped out with his painting commissions, a fact sufficiently memorable to have been handed down in the oral tradition of his Nilsson patrons. Portable

Four long tables, each with a pair of benches, would have provided ample seating for guests invited for Hembygsgården celebrations. As many as a hundred guests would have packed in comfortably. Undoubtedly the Hertmans' wall decorations would have been much admired, each of the painted scenes prettily framed in arched niches with floral topknots, separated by pilasters amusingly reminiscent of garlanded maypoles. The ceiling decoration shows a rather different frondy style – like ostrich feathers.

Baltic blue again underlines the
pensive mood of this corner of the
main living room at
Hembygsgården. A spoon rack
complete with wooden spoons bisects
one of the decorated panels. The
curvaceous clockcase is in a rustic
rococo style. The huge volume
standing open on the table is the
Nilsson family bible.

Painted panel detail from the living room.

scaffolding was erected for the ceiling decoration of the 'big room', and the family marvelled at the sight of Jonas and his wife lying on their backs for days at a stretch brushing in the finely detailed swags, wreaths, and fronds which make up the ceiling scheme, all painted directly onto whitewashed boards in vivid distemper colours.

Family tradition also has it that the big room's decoration was planned to coincide with the wedding of one of the Nilsson daughters to a rich local farmer, which took place in 1774. The date 1765, painted in Roman numerals, close to one of the windows, seems to contradict this. On the other hand, a moment's reflection suggests that it could be the date which is inaccurate, since in 1765 by any reckoning Jonas Hertman was only ten years old! Roman numerals are just the sort of impressive flourish which appealed to rural painters and which they often slipped up over, mis-spellings and mis-datings being both quite common occurrences. An analogous error, this time purely visual, can be found in the handling of the tricky perspective at the foot of the garlanded columns, ambitiously rendered in *trompe-l'oeil*, which fill the spaces between the charming murals in their arched frames, and which in Jonas' perspective are set decidedly askew to their square plinths. Each column sprouted a tiny shelf, now trimmed in crocheted lace, to hold a candle. These, combined with a central candle lantern of the simplest design, must have made the big room at party time radiantly bright relative to most *stuga* interiors; candles, too, were a considerable status symbol at this period.

Jonas (and presumably his wife) also decorated the living room kitchen at Hembygsgården, making eclectic use of motifs which must have seemed impressively up-to-date in late eighteenth-century Edsbyn. Painted swagged drapery – a country version of what we see at Skokloster – runs along the wall behind built-in seating with a second band merely outlined along the blue-painted bench fronts. Painted bands in colour divide the whitewashed walls into 'panels', each one holding a delicate wreath culminating in one of the curious butterfly shapes found in many of the *kurbits* paintings of Dalarna, the province immediately south of Hålsingland. Linseed oil paint, in typically Swedish deep greeny-blue and soft brown red, are used for all the built-in pieces, which include benches, cupboards and dressers, together with wall racks for the display of a magnificent collection of decorated pottery plates. Around these plates Nilsson family history has woven a tale which gives a fascinating insight into the stubborn conservatism of the Swedish peasant class, prosperous or no. When the wall racks were built and painted the family, in all probability – to judge from recorded usage of the day – ate off, and displayed, plates of wood for everyday use, or pewter for best. Much of the time, however, communal meals were dished from a communal bowl or platter, passed round the table, and all present helping themselves with their own spoons. A spoon rack is another feature of the kitchen.

At some unspecified date, probably towards 1830 (the present owner believes her great-grandmother and grandmother were involved, but it could have been her great-great-grandmother and great-grandmother) a young Nilsson wife scandalized the family, but especially her mother-in-law, by splashing out on a whole set of ceramic plates, the first in this fragile though handsome material ever seen in Edsbyn. The outraged matriarch stormed, and threatened to protest against such extravagant folly, but the younger generation evidently won the day, since painted pottery and slipware fills most of one wall, and is also, ironically, one of the most valuable items of furnishing in the place today. It would be interesting to know whether the older lady's outburst was provoked by the shocking novelty of ceramic plates, or by the mundane truth that, compared to everlasting wood and pewter, they were sadly breakable, and thus a potential waste of good kroner. Ceramic work was never very common in northern Sweden due to the lack of workable clay.

And yet, as the vivid rooms at the farm tellingly demonstrate, the Nilssons were no puritans when it came to ostentatious colour and pattern on their walls. The most innovative room scheme to modern eyes, though one squarely part of the fashion of its day, is the 'farmer marbling' used over the upper walls, above the dado, in the small extra parlour – a room dominated by an uncompromising portrait of the present occupiers' grandparents, strong-jawed, unsmiling, and dressed in mourning (or respectable) black. The marbling is painted onto canvas

Marbling with a difference, or 'farmer marbling', enlivens this little parlour with 'stone' shapes as big as giant puffballs. Blue again for dado and stencilled door panels.

hangings stretched over plank walls, implying both that it was an eighteenth-century scheme, and by extension, the work of the Hertmans themselves. As farmer marbling goes, it belongs to the madder variety, immense rounded pebble shapes – reminiscent of marbled papers in the Turkish stone style – roughed out with a mid-blue distemper over whitewash, and lightly detailed in a darker blue scribbly line. Its boldness and scale are entrancing, renewed evidence that a 'faux' finish, in modern parlance, need not be *vraisemblable*, or laboriously worked over, to be stunningly effective as decoration.

Modern marbling makes great play with the softening effects possible with still-wet oil paints and glazes. This farmer marbling, executed in non-manipulable distemper, allowing of no second thoughts or softening, goes for simple certainties, and makes up in attack and directness for what it entirely lacks in finesse. Elsewhere, finesse is not absent in this extraordinary little room, as witness the careful use of toning blues for the stencilled door decoration, and the prettily painted small wall cupboard. The Hembygsgården marbled parlour is a naïve masterpiece, with all the disturbing immediacy of the most memorable primitive paintings, and the more worth preserving since naïve decorative painting is so much less frequently met with, for obvious reasons, than naïve easel art. Interestingly, the style of marbling used here still lives in Sweden today; the tiny *lusthus* at Aelfsunda, recently painted, makes use of precisely the same marbling convention, in the same colours.

A long view of the same room shows more of the typical furnishings of a nineteenth-century Scandinavian parlour. A dragsoffan or pull-out bed stands beside a slightly dilapidated bureau beneath a grim family portrait. Candle sconces and a central lantern provide some illumination. Two decorated regional pieces add a little more colour to a monochrome scene. The dark ceiling is an uncharacteristic addition, guaranteed to minimize daylight one would have thought.

Colour, pattern, and decoration continue unabated through the later, upper storey of Hembygsgården, implying that the Nilsson predilection for colourful display was genetically hardy, and also supplying the modern observer with intriguing documentation of changing tastes and times. Upstairs, the aspirations of the early nineteenth century are enthroned – with one or two retrograde flourishes, such as the immense ceiling roundel on the landing, distantly related to baroque work in grisaille shown elsewhere in this book. By this time wallpaper had become the mark of social status for the Swedish, indeed Scandina-

vian, rural propertied class. Most of the wall treatments, therefore, laboriously imitate by means of stencils, handpainted inch by inch, the repeating patterns which were produced elsewhere on a semi-mechanized or even fully industrialized scale.

Thus, at Hembygsgården, we find a bedroom, the master bedroom in fact, whose peach-pink distempered walls are carefully stencilled with floral motifs on a precise mathematical grid, in white and sludge green, in imitation of some admired but costly or unprocurable wall-paper (Stockholm had its wallpaper factories in the early nineteenth-century, but their output was small and expensive). A boldly coloured – bright blue, beige and dull red – frieze above mimics the fashionable paper border, printed, at this period, in the gaudiest colours. A charming painted long-case clock, probably of an earlier date, stamps the room as Swedish rural, but what made the room habitable, in a northern province only a giant's leap or two south of the Arctic circle, is the simple white ceramic tiled stove rising to ceiling height. Another, lesser, bedroom features a wall treatment of which enough examples survive to suggest that it was once commonplace throughout Sweden. This is *stenkmålning*, or spatter-painting, in white distemper against a background of the distinctive iron-oxide-based soft, dull red used throughout the region. Here it is neatened with a trim stencilled border along the ceiling line, and contrasted with more *stenkmålning* on the dado, in the grey granite mode inaugurated at the Haga Pavilion. Everywhere, as throughout the house, every detail of the furnishings, down to the embroidered linen coverlets, and traditional 'guest towel' hung by the kitchen door remains in accordance with its nineteenth-century blueprint. The sense of stored history is overpowering. The conservatism which made an earlier Nilsson matriarch object to new-fangled ceramic plates must be an important factor in the miraculous teleportation of a complete rural way of life into the late twentieth century.

The present owner, a maiden lady, faithfully maintains her inheritance, in some perplexity as to the relevance of such an undertaking in an altered world. Edsbyn, once a village to which Ovanåker, where Hembygsgården stands, was a satellite hamlet, has grown to suburban proportions, engulfing the farmstead in a typical late twentieth-century splatter of housing, light industry and so forth (though this, being in underpopulated Sweden, is not too threatening). Local conservationists assist her to the best of their ability, the farm buildings are open to visitors at appointed times, collections of old farm implements, and suchlike, are being assembled as bait for tourists. Yet there is a real threat to Hembygsgården implicit in all this, to do with its remoteness from the main tourist caravans, and a misapprehension perhaps of what this magically colourful time capsule represents to the more sensitive and interested observer. What is true of this house is presumably also true of thousands more which have somehow survived, abetted by a dry climate and innate conservatism, in other parts of Scandinavia. One would be loath to see them intensively popularized in the style of guided tours, stopping off for a mid-morning event on their way to the land of nomadic Lapps, yet their survival, as visitable informal museums, seems otherwise problematic.

Like a hovering flying saucer, a painted ceiling roundel on the landing at Hembygsgården represents the last step down the social ladder of a decorative idea inspired by eighteenth-century carved plasterwork. Spatter painting in shades of grey imitates granite, while the wall beyond, distempered a glowing English red, has been spattered with white to create a warmly colourful effect popular all over Sweden.

Another solution, fraught with different problems, is for such places of special interest to be sold – or entrusted, with care-taking responsibilities – to conservation-minded people looking for distinctive holiday homes. In an unprogrammed fashion this is already happening throughout Scandinavia, as an increasingly urbanized, prosperous society begins to look for rural boltholes. Conservationists are constantly approached by second home owners, aware of having acquired more than a shell or a shelter in one of these intensely decorated old cottages, with queries about how to restore them, what to restore, how to restore, with what materials and so forth. The danger is, even given the thoughtful concern of most Scandinavians and the wholehearted efforts of conservation groups and individuals, that what happens in a remote *stuga* on an unvisited rocky promontory miles off the tourist route, seems of little moment to almost anyone anywhere else. And yet our pushy computerized world of faxes and filofaxes needs the stillness, and bedrock stability, of places like Hembygsgården, for reasons both complex and startlingly simple. Merely to be able to say to oneself, in a kaleidoscopically changing environment, that this is how it was once, how our or their ancestors lived and worked, how they liked their surroundings to look, is a necessary, indeed priceless, pause for reflection, a light from the past which throws a long steady beam illuminating in unforeseen and useful ways the here and now.

The spattered red and white bedroom again, showing the rich tweedy texture of this particular wall treatment, and the neat stencilled border. Embroidered coverlets like the one seen here were part of a girl's dowry of household linen, worked and added to over the years. A biblical text is inscribed above a doorway in the room beyond.

FURTHER READING

Fernlund, Siegrun. *Götheborgs Stads Konst-och Målare Enbete.* Stockholm: Bokförlaget Signium, 1983.

Gustaffsen, Gotthard & Björnstad, Arne. *Vården Är Gamla Byggnader.* Stockholm: Bokförlaget Forum, 1981.

Miller, Margaret M. & Aarseth, Sigmund. *Norwegian Rosmaling: Decorative Painting on Wood.* New York: Charles Scribner & Sons, 1973.

Milman, Miriam. *Trompe-l'Oeil Painting: The Illusion of Reality.* New York: Rizzoli International Publications, 1983.

National Museum, Copenhagen, 1980. *Frilands Museet: An Illustrated Guide.*

Nodermann, Maj. *Från Altranstädt Till Delsbo.* Stockholm: Nordiska Museet, 1984.

Nodermann, Maj. *Nordic Folk Art.* Stockholm: Nordiska Museet, 1988.

Nordiska Museet, Stockholm, 1989. *Med Pensel och Schablon.*

Plath, Iona. *The Decorative Arts of Sweden.* Mineola, N.Y.: Dover Publications, 1965.

Strindberg, August. Translated by Schubert, Elspeth H. *The People of Hemsö.* Westport, Conn: Greenwood Press, 1959.

Tunander, Pontus. *Dekorativ Malning.* Västerås: ICA-Förlaget, 1989.

Wooden Architectural Monuments of Transcarpathia. Leningrad: Aurora Art Publishers.

Additional Reading

Dampierre, Florence de. *The Best of Painted Furniture.* New York: Rizzoli International Publications, 1987. London: Weidenfeld & Nicholson, 1987.

Gaynor, Elizabeth. *Finland: Living Design.* New York: Rizzoli International Publications, 1984.

Gaynor, Elizabeth. *Scandinavia: Living Design.* New York: Stewart, Tabori & Chang, 1987. London: Thames & Hudson, 1987.

Groth, Hakan. *Neoclassicism in the North: Swedish Furniture and Interiors 1770–1850.* New York: Rizzoli International Publications, 1990.

INDEX

ACKNOWLEDGEMENTS

The author and publishers wish to thank the following organizations and individuals for their help during the preparation of this book:

Jan Braenne
Elizabeth Hidemark
Swedish National Tourist Board
Pontus Tunander
Volvo Car Corporation

Picture Acknowledgements

All photographs by David George © Cassell except *jacket*, *129* Camera Press, *75*, *77* Norske Folkemuseum, Oslo, *80* Elizabeth Whiting Associates.

Author's Acknowledgements

This book grew out of a hunch that to anyone interested, like myself, in the history and applications of decorative painting, Scandinavia offered surviving examples as varied and surprising as anything to be found in Europe. To find my hunch so lavishly substantiated was a small private delight, but to flesh it out into a book, however modest, required – and received – generous help, encouragement and participation from a great many people. It was my friend Gill de Monpezat who made the remark that first set me thinking. Roger Seamark, Suzanne Martin, Pontus Tunander answered technical questions with angelic patience. Dr Elizabeth Hidemark of the Nordiska Museet, Stockholm, and her colleague, Maj Nodermann, filled out gaps in background knowledge as well as my itinerary. Pernilla Ullberger of the Swedish Tourist Board, and Kurt Nilsson of the Danish Tourist Boards were generous with their time and advice. Ivor and Pat Beresford, Mr and Mrs Jan Weslin, Bertil Wetmark gallantly drove me hundreds of kilometres to chosen locations, as well as feeding me bountifully. La Aberg treated me to one of the best meals I have eaten, anywhere. Decorative painters throughout Scandinavia allowed me to look over their shoulders and watch them at work. I am especially indebted to Jan Braenne, one of Norway's leading conservationist/restorers, for an invaluable resumé of historical decorative materials, tools and practices and their latter day equivalents. Without breakneck translation by Anna George, much valuable information would have been inaccessible, just as without hours of patient information processing by Debenie Morse, many locations might have slipped through our net. But my most heartfelt thanks are due to the good and generous people who really made this book possible by allowing us to invade and photograph their homes – Beatelund, Bjorkesund, Aelfsunda, Ekolssund, Tureholm, Tidö, Sjöo, Steninge, Sandemar, Hembygsgården, a string of decorative 'pearls' every one. David George's photographs went to the heart of every location and his cheerful acceptance of minor problems like fading light or zero temperatures made him an ideal collaborator. My best thanks to him, and Sally Scantlebury who has a rare nose for a good location. Roger Seamark breezed through the practical sections of the book with characteristic aplomb. Lastly, thanks to my editor Christopher Fagg who held my hand and only occasionally slapped my wrist, historian James Ayres of the John Judkyn Foundation, Bath, for challenging my wilder assertions and Liz Haldane for keeping a sharp eye on the logic of it all.

JOCASTA INNES
August 1990